סכות

Tabernacles — Succot

When the Messiah Feasts with Jews and Gentiles

Zaide Reuven

Published by:
Zaide Reuven's Esrog Farm, LLC.

פרדס האתרוגים של סבא ראובן
זיידע ראובן'ס אתרוג-סעדל
PMB 238, 6757 Arapaho Road, Suite 711
Dallas, Texas, 75248

Printed in the United States of America, by Allcraft Printing, Dallas, Texas.

Cover and title page concepts by David Wiseman, illustrated by Luis Martinez, production by Babb Creative, Dallas, Texas.

Zaide Reuven is the *nom de plume* of David Wiseman.

Library of Congress Catalog Card Number: 99-90766

ISBN 0-9666222-1-9

TABLE OF CONTENTS

TABLE OF FIGURES

KEY TO SYMBOLS

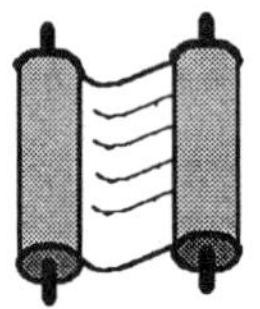

A quotation from the Five Books of Moses

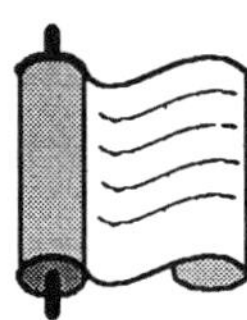

A quotation from the Jewish Prophets or Writings

A quotation from the Jewish Sages

A quotation from the Jewish liturgy, or prayer service

A quotation from the Christian Bible

(This image is used with permission of T/Maker Company, Mountainview, CA)

Except where noted by an asterisk*, all translations of verses from the Jewish Bible are from the ArtScroll Tanach, Mesorah Publications, Brooklyn. The form "Succot" has been used throughout (see *Esrog or Etrog*? page 7).

Quotations from the Christian Bible have been taken from the Authorized King James Version, published by The Gideons International, 1987 edition, with minor adaptations from old English.

For an explanation of the books of the Jewish Bible, see Appendix 2: A Summary of the Jewish Bible and Authorative Sources, page 95.

A Note on Halachic Issues

There are a number of places in this book where I have reviewed Halachot (Jewish Laws) as they relate to Succot. These reviews are intended as general descriptions only and not as authoritative Halachic treatises. One should always consult a Rabbi as to how a Law should be applied in a particular case. Very often the smallest seemingly extraneous detail can alter the way a law is interpreted.

Please treat this book with respect as it contains Torah material

Esrog or Etrog?

In Hebrew, the letter ת (tav) may be pronounced like the letter "T" (Sephardi - Modern Hebrew) or like the letter "S" (Ashkenazi). In most cases, including translated verses from the Jewish Bible, I have used the Sephardi form of words containing this letter. The main exception is for the word "etrog" for which I have used the form "esrog", to be consistent with the name of my company.

Preface

This book is an extension of a previous work on "The Esrog" which has been enthusiastically received by readers throughout the world. During this time I have been approached by a number of Christians interested in purchasing esrog trees and knowing more about the esrog and Succot. Many have wanted to plan events in their communities related to Succot - Tabernacles and the harvest that would provide safe, non-pagan and biblically based alternatives for Halloween.

This caused me to examine the reasons for their interest. I realized at once that a festival such as Succot which had so many messianic associations should be of interest to a faith so concerned with the idea of a messiah, but I was not prepared for the many associations between Succot and Christianity that I did find.

My personal observations on the resurgence of Jewish practice among the Jewish people, the flourishing B'Nai Noach movement and the increasing numbers of converts to Judaism from Christianity led me to suspect that we were witnessing some very special events. Indeed, as the millennium approaches, and mindful of the recent history of the Israel and the Jewish people, there is great anticipation and excitement, not only among Christians, but also among Jews.

This led me to question, from a Jewish perspective, God's purpose for Christianity; and from a Christian perspective, God's purpose for Judaism. A reading of John Hagee's work provided some clue for the latter question, but more importantly, for my own faith, a reading of the Rambam provided what I had suspected was the answer to the former question for some time.

This book is therefore intended for Jewish and Christian audiences, as well as for those who call themselves "Noachides". For my fellow Jews, as well as Noachides, I hope that this book synthesizes our belief in the Messiah in a way that enhances our appreciation and observance of Succot. I hope that this will also encourage you to delve further into the primary sources in a way that could not be replicated here for the sake of brevity.

For Christians, like the many who have already contacted me, I hope that this book presents to you a picture of one of our most precious festivals, ordained by God, a festival that will be celebrated by all truly monotheistic peoples in the messianic era. I do not intend to persuade or cajole you into becoming Jewish, nor do I wish to cause insult or offense. This book is unashamedly written from a Jewish perspective. I have sincerely reported alternative beliefs in a respectful and accurate manner even though I do not agree with them. I hope therefore that you will accept this book in the constructive and instructive manner in which it is intended.

For my wife and family I extend my gratitude for their help and support in this project. I know that our days spent in the succah will be richer as a result.

I once again thank Hashem[1] Who has provided a succah for me in which to study and to grow and to write this book. It is my fervent hope that many will also study, learn, and grow from this book and in their merit, may we witness the coming of the Mashiach ben David and the rebuilding of Jerusalem, speedily and in our days.

כי מצוין תצא תורה ודבר ה" מירושלים

"For out of Zion the Torah will come forth and the word of Hashem from Jerusalem" (Isaiah 2:3)*

David M. Wiseman   דוד אהרן מענדל בן מתתיהו

Ellul 15 5759
August 27 1999

[1] Hashem: God. The four letter name of God is never pronounced, nor is it written, except in Holy objects such as Prayer books, Torah scrolls and the like. Instead the appellation "Hashem" is used, literally "The Name."

ACKNOWLEDGMENTS

It is a pleasure to thank the many individuals who have reviewed my manuscript and provided helpful comments and suggestions, from both Jewish and Christian perspectives. They are Yitzchak Abrams, Pastor Lennie Allen, Rabbi Motty Berger, Menachem and Devorah Brakefield, Charity Dell, Rabbi Bentzi Epstein, Robert and Christine Feith, John Kirkpatrick, Robert and Cheryl Mart, Rabbi Tovia Singer, Mitchell Smith, and Dean Wheelock.

My inclusion of the above names, while intended as a mark of my appreciation does not imply endorsement on their part of any or all of the views that I have expressed herein.

A number of other individuals have been enormously helpful in the production of the book including Gideon and EJ Posner, Lauren Posner and my wife, Lesley. For this support I am truly grateful.

THE AUTHOR

The author is David Wiseman, founder of Zaide Reuven's Esrog Farm. Named after David's grandfather, an avid gardener, Zaide Reuven's Esrog Farm was conceived on Hoshana Rabbah 5755 (1995) in the Dallas Succah of Rabbi Sholley Klein, after the weekly class in Talmud.

Since all present had "taken" the Four Species for the last time, they decided to find out what an esrog tasted like. David wondered what would happen if he planted a few seeds. From these few seeds came a few trees, and from those few trees came the idea to grow more trees. These trees would need a practical guide on how they should be cared for and so David's first book, "The Esrog" was born. This sparked more public interest, and so this book was conceived. Both books have been written under the pseudonym, Zaide Reuven.

When English born David is not tending to his esrog trees or writing about them, David runs a company engaged in medical and pharmaceutical research. David has a Ph.D. in Experimental Pathology and is also a pharmacist. He lives in Dallas with his wife and children.

For my family and for my people

Tabernacles - Succot

When the Messiah Feasts with Jews and Gentiles

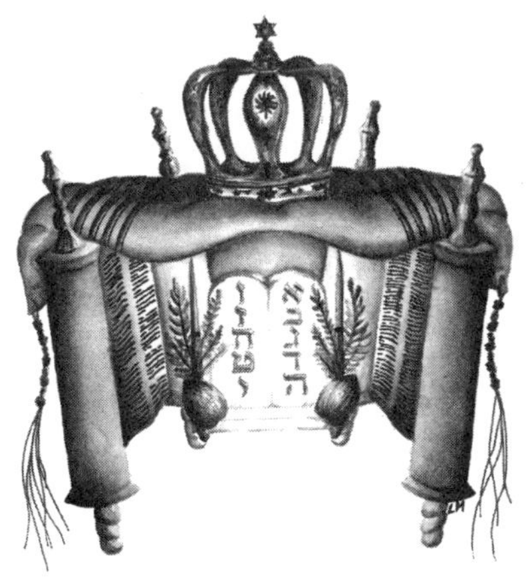

The Four Species

The Four Species showing the central palm branch (lulav), the hadas (myrtle) to its left, and the arava (willow) to its right. The hadas and arava are held with the lulav using a koishekal, made of palm leaves. The esrog (citron) is separate to the left.

CHAPTER 1: SUCCOT: A PICTURE OF THE MESSIANIC ERA

Of the festivals in the Jewish calendar, Succot (Tabernacles) is most closely associated with the messianic era. The prophet Zechariah makes this abundantly clear.[2] After the war of Gog and Magog[3] and the final battle for Jerusalem, when the flesh of Jerusalem's attackers will *"melt away while [they are] standing on [their] feet"* (Zechariah 14:12), the remaining nations of the world will come to Jerusalem at Tabernacles:

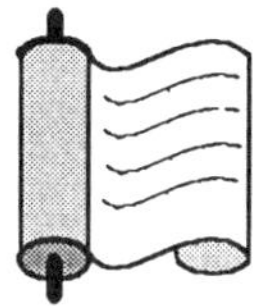

> "It shall be that all those who are left over from the nations who had invaded Jerusalem will come up every year to worship the King Hashem,[4] Master of Legions, and to celebrate the festival of Succot" (Zechariah 14:16).
>
> והיה כל-הנותר מכל-הגוים הבאים על ירושלים
> ועלו מדי שנה בשנה להשתחות למלך ה'
> צבאות ולחג את-חג הסכות

This yearly celebration of Succot in messianic times will be a central event in the life of the world. The Torah emphasizes that the *"nations who will not go up to celebrate the festival of Succot"* will be plagued by a lack of water and punished in this manner (Zechariah 14:18-19).

Let us examine more closely this important festival, ordained by God to be a celebration for the nations of the world, both now and in the messianic era.

---

[2] Chapter 14 of Zechariah is read on the first day of Succot in the synagogue.

[3] See also Ezekial Chapters 38 and 39. It is unclear as to exactly when the Messiah will come in relation to this war. Malachi 3:23 states: *"Behold, I am sending you Elijah before the coming of the great and awesome Day of Hashem."* Elijah will adjure the Jewish people to repent and prepare them for the Redemption. Some opinions hold that Elijah will come immediately before the Messiah, which will be immediately before the war of Gog and Magog. See the excellent article written by Rabbi Dubov at: www.chabad.org/gopher/ideal/live/index.html.

[4] Hashem: God. The four letter name of God is never pronounced, nor is it written, except in Holy objects such as Prayer books, Torah scrolls and the like. Instead the appellation "Hashem" is used, literally "The Name."

CHAPTER 2: SUCCOT: BIBLICAL SOURCES

The four basic commandments relating to Succot are found in Leviticus 23:33–43:

- To Dwell in succot (booths)
- To Take the Four Species
- To Rejoice
- To Assemble in Jerusalem

Succot has four names, reflecting various aspects of the holiday, or scriptural references:

1. Festival of Booths	חג הסכות Chag Hasuccot	Leviticus 23:24
2. Festival of Ingathering	חג האסיף Chag Ha'asif	Exodus 23:16
3. Season of our Rejoicing	זמן שמחתנו Zeman Simchatenu	Deuteronomy 16:14
4. The Feast	חג - Chag	Leviticus 3:39-41

The appointed time for Succot is the 15th Tishri, the seventh month:

"Speak to the Children of Israel, saying: On the fifteenth day of this seventh month is the Festival of Succot, a seven day period for Hashem." (Leviticus 23:34)

דבר אל-בני ישראל לאמר בחמשה עשר יום לחדש
השביעי הזה חג הסכות שבעת ימים לה"

This corresponds to September or October of the secular calendar.[5]

[5] See the entry "Months" in the Glossary, Appendix 1, and Appendix 5, for a list of the civil dates on which Succot falls.

To Dwell in Succot - Booths

The Torah commands us to dwell in booths סכות, temporary structures called succot:[6]

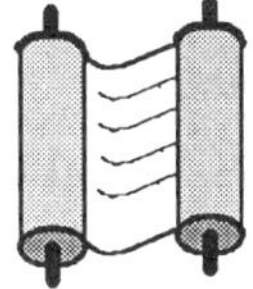

> "You shall dwell in booths for a seven day period; every native in Israel shall dwell in booths. So that your generations will know that I caused the Children of Israel to dwell in booths when I took them from the land of Egypt. I am Hashem, your God." (Leviticus 23:42-43)[7]
>
> בסכות תשבו שבעת ימים כל-האזרח בישראל ישבו
> בסכות: למען ידעו דרתיכם כי בסכות הושבתי
> את-בני ישראל בהוציאי אותם מארץ מצרים
> אני ה" אלקיכם

It is at Succot that the grain is harvested. In Biblical times farm workers lived in temporary huts, or *succot*, in the fields during the harvest. These temporary shelters, booths - succot, were used not only at the time of the grain harvest, but also for other harvests (Isaiah 1:8), to bivouac soldiers (II Samuel 11:11) or to house animals (Genesis 33:17).

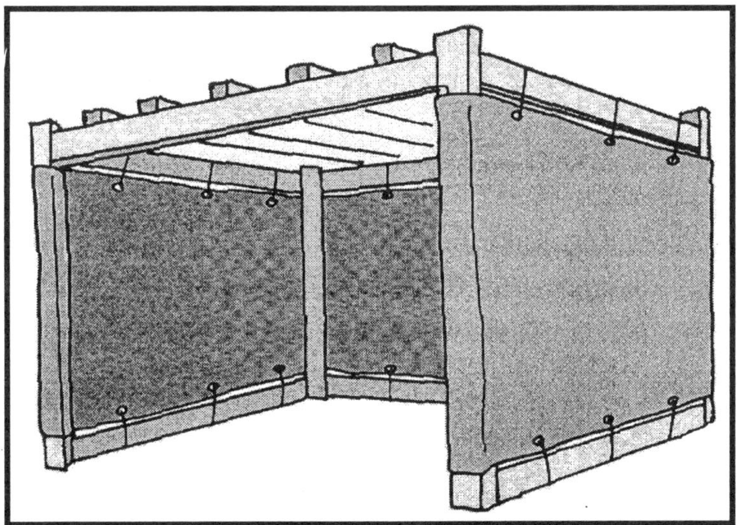

Typical succah seen outside many homes today

---

[6] Succot is the plural form of succah.

[7] Also see Numbers 29:12: *"On the fifteenth day of the seventh month, there shall be a holy convocation for you; you shall do no laborious work, you shall celebrate a festival to Hashem for a seven day period."*

To Take the Four Species: Arba Minim

The Torah commands us to take the Four Species ארבעה מינים:

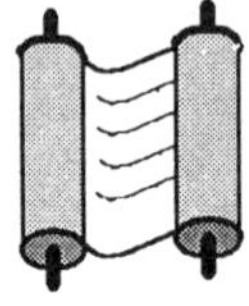

> "And you shall take for yourselves on the first day the fruit of goodly trees, the branches of date palms, twigs of a plaited tree, and brook willows...." (Leviticus 23:40)*
>
> ולקחתם לכם ביום הראשון פרי עץ הדר
> כפת תמרים וענף עץ-עבת וערבי-נחל

The Torah is not explicit in stating the identity of the Four Species shown here. Indeed, according to the Midrash,[8] even the wise King Solomon was unable to identify them from the Torah.[9] However, according to the Rambam (Maimonides)[10] and others, there is an Oral Jewish tradition identifying the fruit of the "Goodly Tree" (Leviticus 23:40) as the esrog-citron since the giving of the Law to Moses in 2448 (c 1313BCE). In recording this tradition the Talmud defines the Four Species as:

Lulav	- Palm branch
Esrog	- Citron - fruit of the goodly tree
Hadas	- Myrtle - three twigs of a plaited tree [11]
Arava	- Willow - two stems

The Four Species

[8] Midrash: Collections of homiletics, parables and moral legends based on the Bible. Part of the Oral Tradition

[9] Midrash: Vayikra Rabbah, Emor 30:15, also cited in Computorah, M. Katz, Achdut Printing, Jerusalem, 1996, pp36

[10] Rambam states that the Four Species were plentiful in the Land of Israel when the Jewish people entered it. Exemplary of the verdure lacking in the desert, the taking of the Four Species served as a joyful reminder of their entry into the Promised Land (Guide of the Perplexed III:43, translated by Pines, S. University of Chicago Press., pp570-574).

[11] Some have the custom to take 4, 12, 13 or 26 myrtle branches (Sefer Haminhagim, Kehot Publication Society, Brooklyn, 1991, p140). Each of these numbers has mystical significance.

To Rejoice

The Torah commands us to rejoice at Succot:

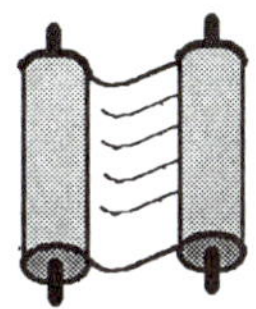

> "...and you shall rejoice before Hashem, your God for a seven day period." (Leviticus 23:40)
>
> ושמחתם לפני ה" אלקיכם שבעת ימים

This command gives rise to one of the epithets for the festival: "Season of our Rejoicing." זמן שמחתנו

To Assemble in Jerusalem

The Festival of Succot is one of the three pilgrimage festivals, when all men must worship at the Temple:

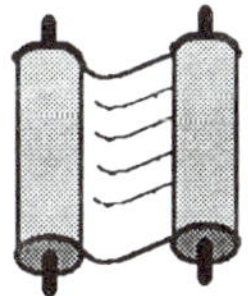

> "Three times a year all your males should appear before Hashem, your God, in the place that You will choose: on the Festival of Matzot [Passover], the Festival of Shavuot [Pentecost], and the Festival of Succot [Tabernacles], and he shall not appear before Hashem empty handed, everyone according to what he can give, according to the blessing that Hashem, your God, gives you." (Deuteronomy 16:16-17)

This commandment cannot be fulfilled until the restoration of the Temple.

CHAPTER 3: PRACTICAL OBSERVANCE OF SUCCOT

Preparation for Succot

Succot begins on the 15th Day of the Hebrew month of Tishri, corresponding to September or October. However, preparation for Succot begins at least several days before. The two most important preparations are:

- Obtaining the Four Species
- Building the Succah

Obtaining the Four Species

Each of the Four Species must conform to minimum requirements as well as additional requirements to add to the beauty of the commandment.

The Four Species (Detail)

Lulav - Palm (with holders) Esrog - Citron

Hadas - Myrtle Arava - willow

The centerpiece of the Four Species is the esrog or citron, the purchase of which is made with the most care and expense. The esrog must be purchased from a reliable source to avoid the use of grafted esrogim, that is fruit which has resulted from the union of one type of tree with another.

The Four Species must neither be borrowed nor stolen. Although the Four Species can be purchased any time before Succot, the pious attempt to buy theirs before Rosh Hashanah, the Jewish New Year, which occurs 14 days earlier. This is so that the merit of having prepared for this commandment will be recorded for them during the period of Judgment between Rosh Hashanah and Yom Kippur (Day of Atonement).

The Four Species should be stored with care when not in use. Keep the esrog in its box. Keep the willow and myrtle with the lulav, but cover them with a lightly dampened cloth wrapped in silver foil. If necessary keep extra willow in water in case the first set spoils.

Building the Succah

The construction of the succah traditionally begins just after Yom Kippur - the Day of Atonement, five days before Succot. Arriving home from Synagogue and before breaking the fast, it is the custom to drive the first stake in the ground. Many families begin their succah construction one or two weeks earlier, as there is much to do to prepare for all the festivals that occur during the month of Tishri.

Building a succah every year is a great family activity involving everyone in this precious mitzvah. Any commandment should be beautified[12] if possible,[13] and each year we think of ways to beautify the succah. Some have a custom to hang examples of the seven species[14] of produce found in Israel (Deuteronomy 8:8) as reminders of God's provision for us. The children draw colorful pictures to hang on the walls, and we hang (plastic) fruit from the support beams. I use esrog trees to adorn our Succah.

During Succot we invite guests to dine with us in the succah. If any of them are not able to have a succah of their own we invite them to help us build the succah beforehand, so that they may share in that part of the mitzvah, commandment. An interesting variant on this theme has been adopted by the Lubavitcher Chasidim. As part of their efforts to enable all Jews to fulfill God's commandments, a Halachically acceptable, traveling

---

[12] Exodus 15:2 states *"This is my God and I will build him a Sanctuary"*. The Talmud (Shabbat 133b) explains from this that we are duty bound to build a beautiful Succah, as well as to beautify other items such as the lulav, a Sefer Torah, a Shofar, and Tzizit (ritual fringes).

[13] Taking care to avoid "adding" to the Torah, since this is a prohibition (Deut. 13:1).

[14] Dates, figs, grapes, olives, wheat, barley and pomegranates

"sukkahmobile"[15] may sometimes been seen in the downtown areas of large cities such as New York. Jewish pedestrians are invited into the succah to fulfill not only this commandment, but also to take the Four Species.

Nowadays, a variety of ready-to-use succah kits can be purchased to accommodate families and budgets of all sizes. Some people, myself included, derive a certain satisfaction from designing and assembling their own "kit." I made my succah kit about nine years ago, and it is still serving our family well, having undergone several enhancements along the way. My basic design is shown in Appendix 4.

Practical Celebration of Succot

Like all Jewish festivals, we celebrate Succot both privately in the home and communally[16] with a minyan, a quorum of 10 men over the age of 13.[17] Preferably an individual should attend communal services.[18] If one is unable to do so, one may pray at home[19] but certain portions of the communal services, such as the reading from the Torah scroll, are omitted.

The dates of Succot in the civil calendar are given in Appendix 5. Like all Jewish Festivals, Succot begins at sundown on the previous evening.

---

[15] Mishnah Succah 2:3

[16] It is preferable that communal services be held in the presence of a Torah scroll, usually housed in a synagogue.

[17] One of the main reasons why 10 men and not 10 women are counted for a minyan is to atone for the sin of the 10 male spies, who by their unfavorable report of their mission incited regret and rebellion in the Children of Israel for having been liberated from Egypt. Contrary to a popular misconception, this in no way reflects a "second class" status of women in Judaism. See footnotes 19 and 65.

[18] The order of services, both communal and at home, are found in the Siddur, the book of daily Jewish prayer. Special adaptations of the Siddur, called machzorim (plural of machzor), are available for each of the main festivals and contain all the readings from the Bible as well as the unique order of prayers said on those occasions. A number of versions are published. The ArtScroll Machzor on Succos is particularly good.

[19] Because of their heavy and important responsibilities in the home, women are exempted from the requirements of time-bound commandments such as the attendance of communal services at set times. Again, contrary to a popular misconception, this in no way reflects a "second class" status of women in Judaism. See also footnotes 17 and 65.

Succot at Home

All seven days of Succot have a special sanctity, but the first two days[20] have a more elevated status akin to that of the Sabbath. Like the Sabbath we refrain from all of the 39 labors used to construct the Tabernacle of the Wilderness, the temporary structure used to house the tablets of the law. Unlike the Sabbath, on Succot (also Pesach and Shavuot) we are permitted to prepare food if it is done from a pre-existing flame. We are also allowed to carry certain essential items in a public domain, and between public and private domains, including of course the Four Species. The remaining days are called "Chol Hamoed" (The Ordinary Days of the Festival).

The festival begins in the home with the lighting of the festival candles. As on the Sabbath two candles are lit, preferably by the woman of the house, at least 18 minutes before sunset[21] The following blessing is recited:

ברוך אתה ה" אלקינו מלך העולם אשר קדשנו במצותיו וצונו להדליק נר של [שבת ושל] יום טוב "Blessed are You Hashem our Lord, King of the Universe Who has sanctified us by Your Commandments, Who has commanded us to kindle the light of [the Sabbath and of][22] the Festival."

On the first two nights of Succot the following is also said:

ברוך אתה ה" אלקינו מלך העולם שהחינו וקימנו והגיענו לזמן הזה "Blessed are You Hashem our Lord, King of the Universe, Who has kept us alive, sustained us, and brought us to this season."

We then recite a special version of the evening prayer (Maariv).

[20] Like Passover (Pesach), Shavuot (Pentecost) and Shemini Atzeret/Simchat Torah (Eighth Day of Solemn Assembly and the Rejoicing of the Law), two days of Succot are observed outside Israel, whereas only one is observed inside Israel. This relates to the times when New Moons were declared upon the testimony of witnesses and messages sent to the Diaspora (Babylonia) by a system of fire signals. Because of the ambiguity of when exactly the New Moon had occurred, two days of the holiday were (and still are) observed outside of Israel.

[21] On the second night of the festival the candles are lit one hour after sunset from an existing flame which was lit prior to lighting the candles of the first night.

[22] This is inserted if the festival coincides with the Sabbath.

On the first and second nights of Succot, and before the meal, we "sanctify" the Festival by reciting the Kiddush[23] (meaning sanctification). Because this is Succot, we do this in the Succah. Traditionally the man of the house chants the following blessing on wine:

ברוך אתה ה" אלקינו מלך העולם בורא פרי הגפן

"Blessed are You Hashem our Lord, King of the Universe Who creates the fruit of the vine"

"Blessed are You Hashem our Lord, King of the Universe, Who has chosen us from every people, exalted us above every tongue, and sanctified us with His commandments. And You gave us Hashem our God, with love, appointed festivals for gladness, festivals and times for joy, Succot, the time of our gladness, a holy convocation, a memorial from the Exodus from Egypt. For You have chosen us and You have sanctified us above all the peoples and Your holy festivals in gladness and in joy have You granted us a heritage. Blessed are You Hashem Who sanctifies Israel and the seasons."

ברוך אתה ה" אלקינו מלך העולם אשר קדשנו במצותיו וצונו לישב בסכה

"Blessed are You Hashem our Lord, King of the Universe Who has sanctified us by Your Commandments, Who has commanded us to dwell in the succah."

ברוך אתה ה" אלקינו מלך העולם שהחינו וקימנו והגיענו לזמן הזה

"Blessed are You Hashem our Lord, King of the Universe, Who has kept us alive, sustained us, and brought us to this season."

As with all meals that include bread, we wash our hands with a special blessing. The blessing for bread is said and the meal is begun. After the meal, we sing the Grace After Meals, with special insertions for Succot.

Dwelling

We dwell in the succah as much as possible, preferably sleeping in it. If this is not possible we eat all our meals in the succah, including snacks. The most festive of these meals are usually dinner on the first and second nights of Succot, lunch on the first and second days of Succot, as well as the meals on the Sabbath that falls during the festival. These are all occasions when family and friends return from the main Synagogue

[23] The Kiddush is modified when the festival coincides with the Sabbath.

services of the festival. An attenuated version of Kiddush is recited before lunch on these days.

On all occasions after we make the appropriate blessing over a meal or snack, we recite the additional blessing of "Layeshev basuccah" (to dwell in the succah):

ברוך אתה ה" אלקינו מלך העולם אשר קדשנו במצותיו וצונו לישב בסכה

"Blessed are You Hashem our Lord, King of the Universe Who has sanctified us by Your Commandments, Who has commanded us to dwell in the succah."

If it is raining hard we may leave the succah to eat, but on the first night, we still say Kiddush (blessing over wine) and eat at least an olive size piece of bread in the succah. There are variant opinions as to what to do on the second night.

Customarily, we hold an additional party in honor of the Simchat Bais HaShoaiva (see page 54). This is usually held on the third through the sixth day of the festival that is not a Sabbath. Many communities hold a "Succah Hop" in which congregants hop from one succah to another in a neighborhood, enjoying a snack and appreciating the variety and ingenuity of succah design.

Ushpizin - Exalted Guests

Another custom is to greet guests into the succah. The "Ushpizin" are the seven guests who are invited on each day. Each day one of the guests takes his turn in leading the others: Abraham[24], Isaac, Jacob, Joseph, Moses, Aaron, and David.[25] Among Sephardim there is the custom to set aside a specially decorated chair for "guest of the day." Another beautiful custom among children is to visit the friends who have the same name as the "guest" for that day. Still another custom, which is certainly meritorious, is to invite seven poor people to eat in the succah.

---

[24] We remember Abraham's invitation of the three angels into his tent (Genesis 18:1).

[25] At a Kabbalistic level these seven guests represent the seven "Sephirot," attributes with which God interacts with creation. These Sephirot are: Lovingkindness (Abraham), Power (Isaac), splendor (Jacob), Eternity (Moses), Glory(Aaron), Foundation (Joseph), and Kingship (David).

Traditional Foods

No description of a Jewish Festival can be complete without discussing the menu. Succot is surprisingly devoid of the traditional foods associated with other festivals: matzo on Passover, dairy food on Shavuot, apple and honey on Rosh Hashanah and latkes on Chanukah.

However, coming close on the heels of Rosh Hashanah and continuing the themes of repentance, judgment, and the hope for a sweet New Year, there is a tradition to continue serving apples and honey and other sweet dishes, such as strudel.

Rosh Hashanah: Apple and Honey, with Shofar

Other foods that have found their way into tradition can be found in the pages of Jewish cookery books. Joan Nathan[26] records a tradition of pumpkin and chick pea soup from Morocco. Despite the "thanksgiving" nature of Succot the pumpkin motif is quite independent of its use in the American holiday of Thanksgiving.

The gathering of the grain harvest at Succot is also cause for the inclusion of a number of grains in Succot dishes. Cabbages stuffed with meat ("holishkes") and grains such as barley, rice, and buckwheat are particularly tasty. Like stuffed cabbages, kreplach (dough stuffed with meat) reminds us of the succah enclosing us within it.

---

[26] Jewish Cooking in America, Joan Nathan, Alfred A Knopf, New York 1998

Anything made from last years esrog is very appropriate for Succot including: esrog jelly, esrog schnapps, and candied esrog peel.[27]

Havdallah

Just as the lighting of the festival (or Sabbath) lights marks the boundary between the Festival (or Sabbath) and the ordinary days that precede it, a

Selection of Esrogim

ceremony called Havdallah[28] (separation) is performed to mark the transition from the sanctity of the Festival to a day of lesser sanctity. The blessing on wine is said over a full cup:

ברוך אתה ה" אלקינו מלך העולם בורא פרי הגפן
"Blessed are You Hashem our Lord, King of the Universe Who creates the fruit of the vine."

followed by the blessing of Hamavdil (separation):

---

[27] For some delicious Esrog recipes see "The Esrog" by Zaide Reuven, Zaide Reuven's Esrog Farm: see page 108.

[28] On the Sabbath an extended version of Havdallah is recited. Following the blessing over wine, a blessing over spices is said (representative of the additional soul given to us on the Sabbath), and a blessing over a multi-wicked candle (representative of man's first act of after the Sabbath in discovering fire). Following the Hamavdil blessing, the candle is extinguished in wine which is spilt onto a dish, and the remainder of the wine drunk from the cup.

ברוך אתה ה" אלקינו מלך העולם המבדיל בין קדש לחול בין אור לחשך בין ישראל לעמים בין יום השביעי לששת ימי המעשה:
ברוך אתה ה" המבדיל בין קדש לחול

"Blessed are You Hashem our Lord, King of the Universe, who separates between holy and secular, between light and darkness, between Israel and the nations, between the seventh day and the six days of labor. Blessed are You Hashem who separates between holy and secular."

Taking the Four Species

Hold the lulav bundle with the spine of the lulav (palm branch) towards you, the arava (willow) on the left and hadas (myrtle) on the right.[29] The tops of the myrtles should be higher than those of the willows. Hold the bundle in the right hand and the esrog (citron) in the left hand[30] with its pitam (protuberance) downwards. Recite the blessing:

ברוך אתה ה" אלקינו מלך העולם אשר קדשנו במצותיו וצונו על נטילת לולב

"Blessed are You Hashem our Lord, King of the Universe Who has sanctified us by Your Commandments, Who has commanded us to take the lulav."

On taking the Four Species for the first time recite the following:

ברוך אתה ה" אלקינו מלך העולם שהחינו וקימנו והגיענו לזמן הזה

"Blessed are You Hashem our Lord, King of the Universe, Who has kept us alive, sustained us, and brought us to this season."

Turn the pitam uppermost. Facing east, hold the lulav and esrog together and wave in the six directions: east (forwards), south (right), west (backwards), north (left), up and down, to symbolize God's omnipresence. At each direction shake the bundle away from the body, then close to the body, repeating this three times before proceeding to the next direction.[31] This ceremony is called "Taking the Four Species," or in Yiddish "bensching lulav and esrog."

---

[29] The bundle is bound together with a holder (koishekal) made from lulav fronds. Rings also made from fronds bind the bundle at the base. Two (according to some opinions, three) rings hold the lulav itself tightly, but loose enough to permit the leaves to rustle when shaken. Some have the custom to use brightly colored ribbons to decorate the lulav.

[30] Reversed for left-handed people

[31] There are variant customs on how the Four Species are taken.

The Four Species can be "taken" in most places, but the succah is perhaps the most appropriate. Many people prefer to perform this commandment in their own succah before attending synagogue. Entering the succah immerses us entirely in the commandment. The Four Species are brought close to us. The esrog, symbolizing the heart, is placed closest to the heart so that the expression of holiness brought about by the performance of this commandment is infused directly into the seat of human emotion. From there it can permeate the entire body, including the intellect. With the total physical immersion (entering the succah), and emotional and intellectual immersion (the Four Species) in the commandments, expressions of God's will, we become one with God's will. The appreciation of this fact results in the unlimited joy referred to in Deuteronomy 16:15.[32]

The Four Species after Succot

Because they have been used for the performance of a Biblical Commandment, the Four Species must not be discarded casually.[33]

Clove-Laden Esrog used for Havdallah Spices

The esrog can be dried or laced with cloves[34]and used as a besamim (spices) for Havdallah[35]. Candied esrog peel is particularly tasty, as is esrog schnapps or jelly.[36] The fragrant leaves of the hadas (myrtle) can be used as spices for Havdallah, and the arava (willow) can be grown for future years. The hadas stems and lulav can be used to search for leaven (Chametz) at Passover, after which they are burned along with the leaven.

---

[32] Likutei Sichos by Rabbi Sholom Ber Wineberg, Sichos in English, Brooklyn
[33] In other words they should not be tossed in the garbage.
[34] Cloves are inserted into the Esrog before it is allowed to dry out.
[35] See *Havdallah*, page 27
[36] See footnote 27

In this way the old Four Species are used in the performance of new commandments.

Succot in the Synagogue

As with all festivals, Synagogue services are centered around the three prayer services conducted every day of the year:

Maariv	The evening prayer said after sundown.
Shacharit	The morning prayer. On Sabbaths, festivals, and Monday and Thursday mornings, this includes a reading from the Torah scroll.
Minchah	The afternoon prayer said before sundown.

These services are said in place of the sacrifices offered at the time of the Temple. On normal weekdays in the morning service, men over 13 wear Tefillin (see Glossary, page 92). These are not worn during the first two days of Succot.[37] Some communities have the custom not to wear them on the other days of Succot either. Other modifications to the Synagogue service are as follows:

Hallel

Immediately following the morning service, we recite Hallel (Praise). This consists essentially of the joyous Psalms 113-118, which are sung with cheerful and popular melodies. During Psalm 118 and at other points during Hallel, the Four Species are waved in the six directions. If one has not already done so, recite the blessings over the Four Species (see Taking the Four Species, page 28) just prior to Hallel.

Piyutim (Liturgical Poems)

Piyutim are recited throughout the Succot services (as on other festivals). These liturgical poems capture the essence of the day and include phrases taken from the scriptures or Talmud. They are often written in acrostic, with the first letters of each stanza spelling out the Hebrew alphabet, or the name of the paytan, the poet.

Groups of piyutim are called by a collective name reflecting their point of insertion into the service. For example, those inserted after the passage in

[37] Tefillin are not worn on Sabbath either. Since tefillin, the Sabbaths and Festivals are a sign of Israel's holiness to God, and only of these is needed on a Festival or Sabbath, tefillin are not worn.

the morning service "yotzer" יוצר אור ובורא חשך (who fashioned light and created darkness), are called "yotzrot".[38]

Readings from the Bible

As on Sabbath and other Festivals, we read publicly from the Bible. The selections from the Pentateuch are read from a Torah scroll. The selections from the Prophets are notable in that they reflect the messianic nature of Succot.

Ecclesiastes - Kohelet

Lest, in the time of such celebration and joy as Succot, we forget our responsibilities to Hashem, we read the book of Kohelet - Ecclesiastes. The message of Solomon's penultimate verse is clear:

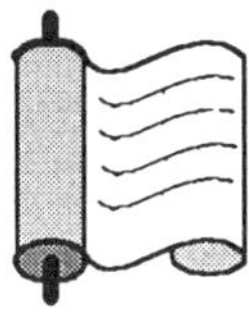

"The sum of the matter, when all has been considered: Fear God and keep His commandments, for that is man's whole duty." (Ecclesiastes 12:13)

סוף דבר הכל נשמע את האלקים ירא
ואת מצותיו שמור כי זה כל האדם

Musaf

Meaning "Additional." Immediately following the reading from the Pentateuch and Prophets, an additional prayer is said on Sabbaths, Festivals and New Moons. This is said in place of the additional sacrifices made in the Temple on these occasions.

Hoshanot

Every day during Succot, after Musaf,[39] we recite the Hoshanot prayers, so called because they begin with the word Hoshana הושענה, meaning "Please save." The Hoshanot prayers have one goal: to obtain salvation for the Jewish People and the rebuilding of the Temple (through the coming of the Messiah).

The Hoshanot recount various attributes of God's greatness and invoke the individual merits of our ancestors or the collective merits of our nation. Hoshanot are recited in a joyous procession (hakafa) around the bima (the

[38] ArtScroll Machzor for Succos, p217

[39] According to Sephardi custom, Hoshanot are recited after Hallel, when congregants already have the Four Species in their hands.

lectern) with the congregants carrying their lulavim and esrogim except on Shabbat (the Sabbath).

This ceremony recalls[40] Temple times when these circuits were made around the Altar. Willow branches eleven cubits[41] long were brought in procession from Motza, a place outside of Jerusalem. They were erected against the sides of the Altar so that they would droop down over it (forming a "succah"). Shofars would be sounded and the altar circled by Cohenim (priests) once a day, and seven times on Hoshana Rabbah. They would chant:

"Please Hashem, save now! Please Hashem, bring success now!"[42]

This would be performed also on Shabbat, but the willows which had been cut prior to Shabbat were placed in golden vessels filled with water so they would not wilt.[43]

Depending on the day of the week and month, different combinations of Hoshanot are recited, but they always end with a resounding recitation of verses from Psalms and Kings:

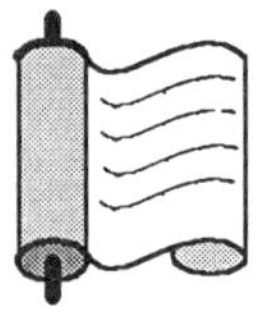

"Save Your nation and bless Your inheritance, tend them and elevate them forever." (Psalms 28:9)

הושיעה את עמך, וברך את נחלתך, ורעם ונשאם עד העולם

"....that He bring about justice for His servant and justice for His people, Israel, each day's need in its day; <u>that all the peoples of the earth shall know that Hashem is God, there is no other</u>." (Kings 1 8:59-60)*

למען דעת כל עמי הארץ, כי ה" הוה האלקים אין עוד

[40] Mishnah Succah 4:5. Babylonian Talmud, Succah 45a

[41] The length of a cubit varies from 18.9" to 22.7", according to opinion.

[42] Psalms 118:25

[43] Mishnah Succah 4:6

Readings from the Bible During Succot, Shemini Atzeret and Simchat Torah

DAY	PENTATEUCH	MAFTIR[44]	HAFTARAH[45]
1	Lev 22:26-23:44 Pilgrim festivals	Num 29:12-16 Day 1 sacrifices	Zech 14:1-21 Final battle for Jerusalem. Nations celebrate Succot
2	Lev 22:26-23:44 Pilgrim festivals	Num 29:12-16 Day 1 sacrifices	1 Kings 8:2-21 Solomon dedicates Temple
3: Chol Hamoed[46] 1	Num 29:17-25 Day 2-4 sacrifices		
4: Chol Hamoed 2	Num 29:20-28 Day 3-5 sacrifices		
5: Chol Hamoed 3	Num 29:23-31 Day 4-6 sacrifices		
6: Chol Hamoed 4	Num 29:26-34 Day 5-7 sacrifices		
Sabbath Chol Hamoed	Ex 33:12-34:26[47] Partial revelation of God to Moses, 2nd tablets, 13 Attributes of Mercy, pilgrim festivals	Num 29[48] Ecclesiastes[49]	Ezek 38:18-39:16 Wars of Gog and Magog
7: Hoshana Rabbah	Num 29:26-34 Day 5-7 sacrifices		
Shemini Atzeret	Deut 14:22-16:17 2nd tithe, sabbatical year loan remission, pilgrim festivals	Num 29:35-30:1 8th day Solemn Assembly	1 Kings 8:54-9:1 Solomon's blessing and offerings at Temple dedication
Simchat Torah (evening)	Deut 33:1-26 Blessing of Moses		
Simchat Torah (morning)	Deut 33:1-34:12 Blessing of Moses Death of Moses	Num 29:35-30:1 8th day Solemn Assembly	Josh 1:1-18 Joshua assumes leadership
	Gen 1:1-2:3 - Creation		

44 Additional reading of the Pentateuch preceding the reading from the Prophets

45 Reading from the Prophets was instituted by the Hasmoneans (c.165BCE) to circumvent the ban imposed by the Assyrian-Greeks on the weekly or Festival reading from the Pentateuch. Passages were selected to reflect the scheduled Pentateuchal reading. This continued after the ban was no longer in force.

46 "Ordinary days of the Festival." Unlike the first two days of Succot (one day in Israel) where most of the Sabbath-related laws apply, some restrictions are relaxed during Chol Hamoed. We still dwell in a succah and take the Four Species.

47 Also read on Sabbath Chol Hamoed for Passover

48 The verses read depend on which day of Succot the Sabbath falls

49 If all the days of Chol Hamoed fall during the week, Ecclesiastes is read on Shemini Atzeret. It is read between the morning and additional services.

Hoshana Rabbah "The Great Hoshana"

The seventh day of Succot is called Hoshana Rabbah, "The Great Hoshana," because of the additional Hoshanot that are recited and seven circuits (hakafot) are made, with all the Torah scrolls.

Unlike the preceding days when selected Hoshanot are recited, all Hoshana prayers are recited on Hoshana Rabbah. Unlike the preceding days when only one Torah scroll is removed from the ark, all the scrolls are removed. And unlike the preceding days, seven processional circuits are made around the Bima (lectern).

Exquisitely poetic prayers are added asking for salvation, our return to Zion and the rebuilding of the Temple. We ask for rain by invoking the merit of our ancestors who underwent various trials involving water:

- The Twelve Tribes and their passage through the Sea of Reeds
- Moses who struck the rock which provided water
- The priests who perform the water libation
- The faithful who take the Four Species, planted near water

After the prayers for rain we proclaim our faith in the Revival of the Dead[50] after the coming of the Messiah. As on previous days the Hoshana service concludes with a joyous recitation of the verses from Psalms (28:9) and Kings (I 8:59-60).

The lulav and esrog are put aside for the last time and the Torah Scrolls returned to the Ark which is closed. Finally, bundles of five willow (aravot) branches are beaten on the ground until all the leaves are removed. The reason for this practice is not fully known other than that the prophets performed it in the time of the Temple, and we perform it as a reminder of the Temple.

Two main ideas have been advanced regarding the willows: just as the willow has neither taste (performance of the commandments) or smell (good deeds), the celebrant recognizes he is lacking in these qualities and resolves to remedy his status. A related reason for the willow beating[51] has to do with the process of judgment. Although we are judged on Rosh

---

[50] Based on the Talmud: *"Greater is the day of the rains than the resuscitation of the dead. The resuscitation will benefit only the righteous, but the rains benefit both the righteous and the wicked."* Babylonian Talmud: Taanit 7a.

[51] ArtScroll Machzor for Succos, pXXVI

Hashanah, and our verdict sealed on Yom Kippur, the sentence is not ratified until Hoshana Rabbah when the Heavenly Court has considered all mitigating circumstances, any grounds for mercy and the remorse and repentance demonstrated by the defendant. The beating of the willows represents the expurgation of sin and the "tearing up" of the verdict.

Paradoxically, the arava means willow or wilderness but alludes to the highest of the spiritual realms (Psalms 68:5). As part of the Four Species (see Understanding the Four Species, page 42), the willow is both the Jew who lacks learning and good deeds, as well as the lips, instruments of prayer and of teaching. Thus, the prominence of the willow on Hoshana Rabbah instructs us in the importance of prayer and teaching, through which even the simplest of Jews can attain the loftiest heights.[52] Furthermore, in case one is carried away with the splendor of the esrog in all its perfection, perhaps the purpose of the willows on Hoshana Rabbah is to remind us not to neglect, or cast away those Jews lacking in learning and good deeds.

The Eighth Day of Solemn Assembly (Shemini Atzeret)

The eighth day is a separate festival known as "The Eighth Day of Solemn Assembly" or Shemini Atzeret (Leviticus 23:36). The Four Species were already set aside on Hoshana Rabbah, but some have the custom to remain in the succah, but without reciting the blessing. The day is likened to a party that a father holds for his family. After the party he wishes his family to stay for one more day before departing. In Israel this day is combined with Simchat Torah. Outside of Israel, these two days are observed separately.[53]

A fascinating insight on Shemini Atzeret/Simchat Torah is given in the ArtScroll Machzor.[54] On Shemini Atzeret there is no longer the succah to provide a "shelter of faith", and there is no longer the beautiful commandment of the Four Species to cling to, and to remind us of our national and spiritual unity. So what is left? The Torah, our inherited instrument of Divine Revelation, in which we find protection and unity. Thus Shemini Atzeret/Simchat Torah is a celebration of the Torah, with us today as it was our ancestors.

---

[52] ArtScroll Machzor for Succos, pXXIX

[53] See footnote 20

[54] ArtScroll Machzor for Succos, pXXIV

The Yizkor (Memorial Service) for the Departed is recited on Shemini Atzeret just before the Musaf (Additional) service. During the Musaf, the Prayer for Rain is recited.

From the Musaf (Additional Service) of Shemini Atzeret up until and including the Musaf of the first day of Pesach we insert the phrase:

"Who makes the wind blow and the rain descend"
משיב הרוח ומוריד הגשם

This mentions to God, as it were, our hope that He will send the rains needed over the winter season. We do not begin this insertion prior to Shemini Atzeret because to do so would invite the possibility of rain interfering with the commandment of dwelling in the Succah.

The Rejoicing of the Law (Simchat Torah)

Simchat Torah, The Rejoicing of the Law, marks the end of the yearly cycle of readings from the Five Books of Moses.

A buzz of excitement fills the synagogue on the inaugural evening of Simchat Torah, in anticipation of a great celebration. Children arrive with flags adorned with apples (on the flag stem). In bygone days small candles would be embedded into the apple.

After the main part of the service[55] selected scriptural verses are chanted by individuals who are chosen to be honored.[56] These verses emphasize our yearning for the time when we will celebrate Simchat Torah in the Temple. The celebration is thrown into high gear as these introductory verses conclude with Isaiah's prophesy:

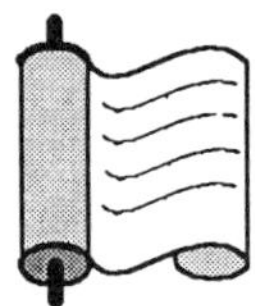

"For out of Zion the Torah will come forth and the word of Hashem from Jerusalem." (Isaiah 2:3)*

כי מציון תצא תורה ודבר ה" מירושלים

[55] Even outside Israel some communities also conduct this celebration on the night of Shemini Atzeret.

[56] Some synagogues have the custom of "auctioning" these honors, to raise money for a charitable cause.

Opening the Ark, all the Torah scrolls are removed. Seven processional circuits ("hakafot") are made around the bima, the central lectern. Individuals are honored to lead each circuit by holding the foremost Torah scroll and chanting various verses and prayers reminiscent of the Hoshanot chanted during Succot. The first chant is:

> Please Hashem, save now!
> Please Hashem, bring success now![57]
> Please Hashem, answer us on the day we call![58]
> God of the spirits,[59] save now!
> Tester of hearts,[60] bring success now!
> O Powerful Redeemer,[61] answer us on the day we call![62]

Much singing and dancing accompanies each Hakafa (circuit), often into the street and around neighborhoods. Every man is given the privilege to hold one of the Torah scrolls and to dance with it, for it belongs to every Jew, young and old, rich and poor, scholar or ignoramus. If a synagogue has many Torah scrolls, they may find themselves leading different groups of celebrants around sections of the synagogue or its environs. Lasting several hours the festivities are sustained by tables of food and drink. In neighborhoods with several synagogues, the celebrants from one synagogue often visit with those from another.

At the end of the seven circuits (Hakafot), all the Torah scrolls are returned to the Ark except one from which the last two chapters of Deuteronomy are read. On the evening of Simchat Torah, the service ends shortly thereafter and a tired congregation returns home to muster up strength for the next morning.

Between the morning and additional service[63], the processional circuits are repeated. When the Torah scrolls[64] are finally returned to the Ark, the last

---

[57] Psalms 118:25
[58] Psalms 20:10
[59] Numbers 27:16
[60] Psalms 7:10
[61] Jeremiah 50:34
[62] ArtScroll Siddur, p761, Mesorah Publications, New York.
[63] Some synagogues have the custom that the protracted celebratory portion of the services take places after the additional services has been said and after a communal lunch.
[64] On the morning of Simchat Torah, it is preferable to retain three Torah scrolls which have been wound prior to the holiday to the appropriate places for the reading of

portion of Deuteronomy (until 33:26) is read in five sections and every male is honored by being called up (aliya) to the Torah.[65] These sections are repeated over until every man has been called. If the congregation is extremely large, Torah scrolls are taken into adjoining rooms for simultaneous readings. The completion of his "aliya" (calling-up) is often marked by a celebratory draught of a suitable beverage. Some synagogues have the custom of also calling up boys under the age of 13 who are able to recite the blessings.

After all the men have been called, the congregants gather in the main sanctuary and all the younger boys are now called up collectively. This is called Kol Hanarim כל הנערים - "All the Young Boys." One or more Tallisim (prayer shawls) are held over the heads of the boys (like a "succah" of God's glory) as the congregation gathers around the bima (lectern). A respected elder is called to recite the blessings on their behalf over the penultimate section of Deuteronomy (33:22-26). This is another great honor. The congregation then recites the blessings over the children from Genesis 48:16 as well as the priestly blessing (Numbers 6:24-26).

The honor of reciting the blessings over the final section of Deuteronomy (33:27-34:12) is given to the "Bridegroom of the Law" (Chatan Torah). Commonly this is an honor that a congregation bestows on one of its esteemed members. In some cases, the Chatan Torah serves an honorary function in the synagogue for the following year. Other congregations auction this honor as a means to raise funds for a charitable cause. To

---

the last portion of Deuteronomy, the Maftir (Num 29:35-30:1), and the first portion of Genesis.

[65] Whenever the Torah scroll is read in public, the portion is divided into a number of sections called Aliyot (pl. aliya - meaning to go up). A man over the age of 13 is called to recite blessings before and after the reading of each section. This is considered a great honor because they are reciting the blessing that enables the public recitation of the word of God. Depending on the sanctity of the day (Weekday =3, New Month = 4, Festival = 5, Yom Kippur = 6, Shabbat =7) the portions are divided into a different number of sections.

In Orthodox synagogues only men over the age of 13 are called to the Torah. Women are not called for two main reason. Firstly it is a violation of the dignity of a Jewish women to be on "public" display. Secondly, because women are exempt from time-bound commandments (including the hearing of the Torah reading), they cannot take away the opportunity of any man present to fulfill a commandment that he is required to keep, even though it is meritorious for a woman to hear the recitation of the Torah. Contrary to popular misconception, this practice not only does not demean woman, but is actually intended to recognize and celebrate their exalted status. See also footnotes 17 and 19.

introduce the calling-up of this person, a special blessing is recited by the gabbai (sexton) of the synagogue.

As at the conclusion of the reading of the final portion of any of the Five Books of Moses, the congregation declares:

חזק חזק ונתחזק "Be strong! Be strong! And Be strengthened!"

Torah Scrolls

Torah scroll in velvet mantle (Ashkenazi)

Torah scroll in gilded case (Sephardi)

No sooner do we conclude the learning of God's Torah, do we begin again to proclaim its infinite nature and our eagerness to learn from it. The honor of reciting the blessings for the first portion of Genesis (1:1-2:3) is given to the "Bridegroom of Genesis" (Chatan Bereshit), chosen in the same fashion as the Chatan Torah. As the Baal Koreh, the person who reads from the Torah, reaches the verse which concludes the events of each day of Creation, the congregation recites in unison that verse, for example:

"And there was evening and there was morning, one day" (Genesis 1:5)

ויהי-ערב ויהי-בקר יום אחד

The congregation also recites in unison the entire section dealing the Sabbath (Genesis 2:1-3). Finally, the Haftarah (reading from the Prophets) is read. Signifying the continuous nature of Torah, the reading is taken from the first section of the Prophets, Joshua 1:1-18.

The service concludes in the normal fashion with the return of the Torah to the Ark and the final prayers and Psalms.

Understanding the Succah

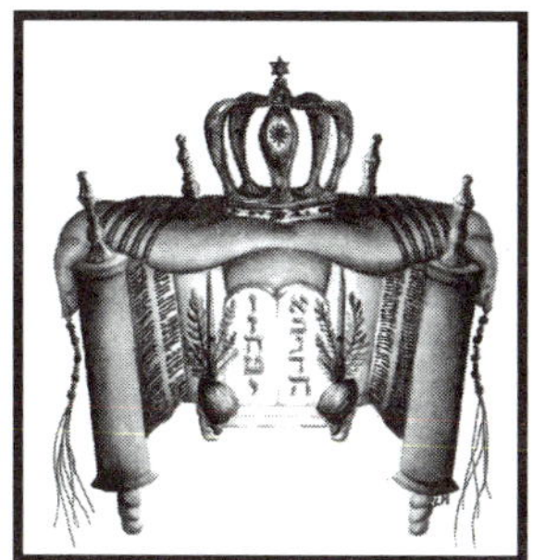

The succah is a wonderful, indeed appropriate, place for quiet meditation and study. There is something quite mystical and tranquil in the temporary space that is created. There are only two commandments that we can perform with our entire bodies, even while asleep: the first is the commandment of dwelling in Israel. The second is the commandment to dwell in the succah. The Temple is sometimes referred to as The Succah. Therefore by building a succah we are, in a sense, creating a miniature of the Temple, the place where the Shechinah - God's presence - can dwell and cover a person sitting in it.[66] By entering the succah, we are abandoning our reliance on the physical in favor of the spiritual and in a sense experiencing what it is like to bath in the Divine Presence. This then is a small taste of the peace that will endure in the messianic era.

In building the succah, our home becomes God's home. In a sense, the succah is the wedding canopy (chupa), under which the joyous union of Hashem (groom) and bride (Israel) can take place. Just as the wedding feasts (Sheva Brachot) last for seven days, so too does Succot. Just as there are guests at the wedding feast, so too do we invite the seven exalted guests (Ushpizin) together with family and friends who can eat, sing and learn together. The succah reminds us of a time when we lived in the desert, and that there are people who have no permanent homes. In the merit of having invited those who have little means to provide their own succah or meals, one is deserving of the presence of the Ushpizin.

The temporary nature of the succah affirms our belief in Divine Mercy, that everyday shelter and sustenance is provided for by none other than Hashem. The Zohar refers to this concept as צלא דמהימנותא "the shelter of faith".[67] Dwelling in the succah affirms not only this belief but also our trust in Hashem that He will provide this protection, just as he did for our ancestors. The message is as relevant for the wealthy as it is for the

[66] Weissman, p328

[67] ArtScroll Machzor for Succos, pXXII

poor. The succah warns the wealthy to remember by Whom his wealth was bestowed, and provides comfort to the poor to trust in Hashem.[68]

A famous question is asked as to why we build the succah in the fall? Since it is related to God's protection of us in the desert, why do we not build the succah in the spring (at the time of Passover) or the summer (at the time of Shavuot - Pentecost)? We build the succah in the autumn, when most people are going into the warmth of their houses, once again to affirm our belief in Divine Protection, as the Psalmist declares:

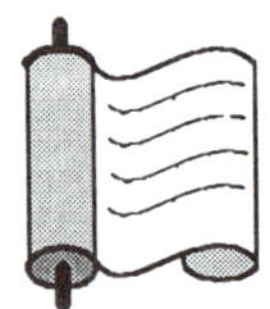

"He will hide me in His shelter (succah) on the day of evil." (Psalms 27:5)

כי יצפנני בסכה בוים רעה

Understanding the Four Species[69]

The sight of these particularly beautiful flora is pleasing and enhances the joy mandatory for the festival of Succot.[70] All Four Species flourish in the vicinity of water. By performing the commandment of the Four Species, God rewards us with rain. The waving of the Four Species back and forth serves to restrain harmful winds; their waving up and down serves to restrain harmful dews.

The commandment of the Succah and of taking the Four Species is so precious to God that the Midrash[71] explains the dialogue between God and the Jewish People in the verse, *"Behold you are beautiful My beloved, behold you are beautiful"* as *"Behold you are fair with the succah, behold you are fair with the lulav and esrog"* (Song of Songs 1:15).

The Four Species and the Jewish Patriarchs

At least two interpretations[72] relate to figures in Jewish history worthy of emulation. In the first of these, the three hadasim (myrtle branches) refer

---

68 ArtScroll Machzor for Succos, citing Rabbi Samson Raphael Hirsch, pXXI

69 Much of this material is taken from "The Esrog", also by Zaide Reuven., see p108

70 Chinuch, Arbarbanel, cited in Weissman, pp330.

71 Midrash Rabbah: Song of Songs 1:15. The lulav and esrog are highlighted together with other significant mitzvot such as tithing, circumcision, tefillin, mezuzah, and tzitzit.

72 Midrash: Vayikra Rabbah 30:10; Weissman, 1982, pp332; Succos, Mesorah, pp58.

to the Three Patriarchs, the two aravot (willow branches) refer to Moses and Aaron, the lulav refers to Joseph and the esrog to King David. The second interpretation is as follows:

Esrog	Abraham and Sara	Just as the esrog is a "beautiful fruit", so too were Abraham and Sara beautified with old age and earthly blessing.
Lulav	Isaac	Another name for the lulav is *kappas* (tied) *temarim*, Isaac being tied to the alter by Abraham.
	Rebecca	Just as the lulav is from the date-palm with its tasty fruit and sharp-pointed leaves, so too did Rebecca give birth to a tzaddik - a righteous person (Jacob) and a rasha - a wicked person (Esau).
Hadas	Jacob and Leah	Just as the hadas has many leaves, so too Jacob had many sons, and Leah the most children of all the matriarchs.
Arava	Joseph and Rachel	Just as the arava withers before the other species, so too did Joseph die before his brothers and Rachel before her sister Leah.

The Four Species and the Human Body

A number of interpretations of the Four Species relate to parts of the human body which they resemble and with which we are to serve God:[73]

Lulav	the spine	we should be upright.
Hadas	the eyes	we should be enlightened and not pursue evil sights.
Arava	the lips	our lips should be used for kind words and prayer and not for evil speech.
Esrog	the heart	the seat of emotions, understanding, wisdom and actions. Just as we choose a perfect esrog, so too must our emotions and actions be perfected.

By holding all Four Species together, we unite all our organs in the service of God. The performance of the mitzvah of lulav and esrog, atones for the sins committed with different parts of our body.

---

[73] Midrash: Vayikra Rabbah 30:14 and Succos, Mesorah pp56.

The connection between the Four Species, or at least the esrog, and the body is further illustrated by the fact that the same type of blemishes that render an animal a *Treifah* (non-kosher, unfit for eating), also render an esrog invalid.[74]

The Four Species and Jewish Festivals

The Four Species can represent the four fall holidays:[75]

Lulav:	Rosh Hashanah:	Just as the lulav represents the potential of the fruit of the date-palm, but not its actuality, so too does Rosh Hashanah represent the potential of our relationship with God.
Esrog:	Yom Kippur:	Just as the esrog is perfect in all ways (taste and smell), so too is our relationship with God perfect after we have made T'shuva (repentance) at Yom Kippur.
Hadas:	Succot:	Three myrtle branches, each with trios of leaves up its branch represent the three major mitzvot of Succot: lulav, succah and simcha (joy). Isaiah (55:13) promises the repentant Israel in the messianic age that "*in place of the nettle, the myrtle will rise*".
Arava:	Simchat Torah: /Shemini Atzeret	Just as the arava has neither taste or smell, there are no biblical commandments concerning these holidays. There are however many customs.

The Four Species and God's Name

The Four Species also represents the four-letter name of God. Holding the Four Species together represents the Unity of God's Name.[76] This is reflected in the kabbalistic declaration recited before taking the Four Species:

---

[74] Babylonian Talmud, Succah 36a.

[75] Attributed by Rabbi D. Gottlieb to his teacher. Lecture: Inner Dimensions of Simcha on Succot. Ohr Somayach Lecture Series, Jerusalem.

[76] Succos, Mesorah pp57.

The Midrash[78] describes how each of the Four Species symbolizes attributes of God, based on the common occurrence of certain key words in Scriptural verses which describe God. For the esrog, the word *hadar* from the injunctive verse regarding the esrog (*"fruit of the goodly (hadar) tree*"- Lev 23:40), also appears in Psalms[79] as follows:

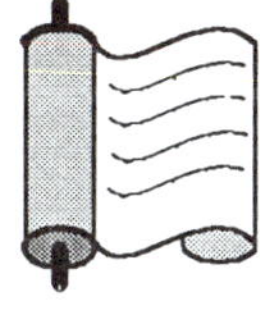

"Bless Hashem, O my soul, Hashem, my God. You are very great; You have donned glory and majesty." (Psalms 104:1)

ברכי נפשי את-ה" ה" אלקי גדלת מאד הוד והדר לבשת

The Four Species and the Unity of the Jewish People

This aspect is discussed more fully under "Succot: Unity and Harmony within Israel" below (page 59).

Symbolism of the Esrog

As the centerpiece of the Four Species, the esrog itself has much symbolism.[80] Believed to be the fruit of the Tree of Knowledge of Good and Evil, in the Garden of Eden, the taking of the esrog in particular atones for the sin of Adam and Eve. For women there are a number of traditions regarding the esrog related to Eve's role in the sin. These relate to the enhancement of fertility, easing the pain of pregnancy and childbirth, fertility and the production of worthy offspring.

Based on the perfection of the esrog and its central role in Succot, the esrog has been a symbol of Jewish Messianic aspirations. For example the esrog appeared on coins of both the First (69-70CE) and Second (132-135CE) Revolts against the Romans.

---

[77] The ArtScroll Machzor for Succos, pp287

[78] Midrash: Vayikra Rabbah 30:9. See also Ramban: Kohelet; Chavel, pp151.

[79] See also Isaiah 63:1 and Psalms 96:6

[80] For an extensive discussion, see "The Esrog" by Zaide Reuven - details on page 108

CHAPTER 5: ELEMENTS OF THE MESSIANIC AGE

The celebration of Succot goes well beyond the celebration of the harvest gathering (Leviticus 23:39), the remembrance of the Exodus from Egypt, and the journey through the desert.

Just as the annual celebration of Succot marks the end of the agricultural year, when the fruits of man's labor may be enjoyed, so too will Succot of the messianic age mark the time when the fruit of man's spiritual labors will be enjoyed for eternity.

For the Jewish People, Succot commemorates not only the time when we lived in desert booths, but also the level of spiritual perfection which that time represented. We yearn to return to those heights, and hope that it will be easier for us to do so since we know we are capable of it. Thus, Succot represents not only a restatement of an achievable spiritual goal that will be reached on Succot of the messianic age,[81] but also a rehearsal of the events of the messianic age itself:[82]

- The war of Gog and Magog will take place.
- The Jewish People will return to observe the laws of the Torah.
- The Temple will be rebuilt.
- The Jewish people will be redeemed and the exiles returned to Israel.
- The nations of the world will recognize and worship the One true God, together.
- There will be an age of prosperity.
- There will be an age of eternal peace and true knowledge of God.
- There will be the Final Judgment and Resuscitation of the Dead.

---

[81] ArtScroll Machzor for Succos, citing the Sfas Emes, pXX.

[82] For a brief description of the Biblical depiction of the messianic age, see Appendix 3. The coming of the Messiah and the events that follow are summarized in Chapters 11 & 12 of Hilchos Melachim (Laws of Kings) from the Mishneh Torah of the Rambam (see www.chabad.org/rmbm1112.htm; also www.j4j.addr.com/nojavasite/webdocs/messiah.html). There are variant opinions on the sequence and type of events (see Babylonian Talmud, Megillah 17b-18a; Sanhedrin, Chapter 11). The Appendix in the ArtScroll Talmud, Tractate Sanhedrin volume 3 entitled "The Messianic Era, Resurrection and the World to Come" is worth reading.

Let us examine how each event is reflected in the Festival of Succot.

The War of Gog and Magog will Take Place

At the beginning of the messianic age, the Wars of Gog and Magog will take place (Ezekial 38:18-39:16, read on Succot).[83] The identity of these combatants has been the subject of great speculation, but Gog will lead an attack against Israel which will kindle Hashem's wrath, His judgment on the nations and His ingathering of Israel. Ezekial tells us what will happen:

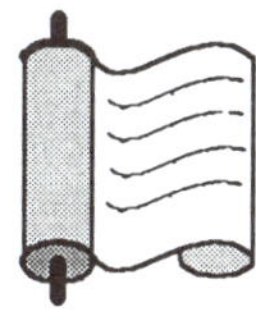

> "It will be at the End of Days that I will bring you upon My land, in order that the nations may know Me, when I become sanctified through you before their eyes....It shall be on that day that on the day that Gog comes against the soil of Israel.....My raging anger will flare up.....I will be exalted and I will be sanctified, and I will make Myself known before the eyes of many nations; then they will know that I am Hashem" (Ezekial 38:16-23).

Here we see that God's purpose for bringing Gog to the Land of Israel, is for the nations to know Hashem (Ezekial 38:16). This is in a time of war. Contrast this with the nations coming to Jerusalem in the peace that will follow the coming of the Messiah (Zechariah 14:16). We can thus see why these selections from both Ezekial and Zechariah are read on Succot.

A more abstract explanation of these passages comes from an understanding of the word Gog גוג, meaning "roof," a symbol of everything materialistic, of modern man's belief in his self-importance and arrogance. In the messianic era, this false faith will be destroyed and we will realize that there is only one source of our protection, namely God. Succot then teaches us that *"our apparently flimsy roofs will ultimately be triumphant over modern man's misguided sense of security."* [84]

The Jewish People will Return to Observe the Laws of the Torah

Our holy writings state clearly that only when a man from the House of David comes, brings about the ingathering of the Jewish exiles, the rebuilding of the Temple, the establishment of world peace, resurrection of

---

[83] The Talmud (Megillah 17b, Sanhedrin 97a) describes the seven years that will precede the Messiah. In the first year there will be famine in some areas. In the seventh year wars will break out, and at the end of this year the Messiah will come.

[84] Rabbi Reuven Lauffer, Ohr Somayach, www.virtual.co.il./city_services/holidays/sukkot-8Atzeret/gems.htm

the dead and the universal knowledge of God, will we know that the Messiah has come and the messianic age is upon us.[85]

One of the prerequisites for the declaration of the Messiah is the return by all the Jewish People to the Torah.[86] How then do we relate this to Succot? The festival of Succot falls on the 15th day of the Hebrew month of Tishri, approximately September or October. Five days before is Yom Kippur, the Day of Atonement, when Jews complete their repentance and atonement for previous sins. Only in such a spiritually elevated state can they look forward to a New Year of an elevated existence closer to Hashem, joyously celebrated during Succot.

Having repented and atoned, and to signify a renewed resolve to observe the commandments of the Torah, Jews speed home after Yom Kippur to begin construction of the succah. Indeed it has been argued[87] that the two portrayals of the succah (i.e. the temporary dwellings in the wilderness and the "Clouds of Glory") represent the two levels of repentance described in the Zohar:[88] The lower form (teshuvah tata'ah) is for a specific transgression or group of transgressions, and a higher form (teshuvah ila'ah) is an uplifting of the entire personality, a total ennobling of one's direction in life. While we need to accomplish the former, our aspiration to the latter will be realized in the messianic age.

Rabbi Shlomo Riskin[89] synthesizes the idea of repentance with the succah further by citing the Laws of Repentance[90] in which *"exile serves as a forgiveness for sin in that it causes a person to become more subdued, humble and subservient.*" What could be more humbling than for someone to no longer have a permanent roof over his head? The succah then is a symbol of this exile, this repentance and forgiveness that is the source of joy. Through repentance the penitent achieves a state of perfection and is

---

[85] Ezekial 37. See also Rambam, Hilchos Melachim 11:4 for a discussion of the criteria for the declaration of the Messiah.

[86] Sadly, for a variety of reasons there are some Jews who know little of the gift gave them by God.

[87] Rabbi Shlomo Riskin, Ohr Torah, Efrat, Israel. www.virtual.co.il./city_services/holidays/sukkot-8Atzeret/riskin.htm

[88] Zohar: the mystical writings

[89] Rabbi Shlomo Riskin, Ohr Torah Institutions, Efrat, Israel, www.virtual.co.il./city_services/holidays/sukkot-8Atzeret/riskin.htm

[90] Rambam, Mishneh Torah, Laws of Repentance, 2:4

drawn close to the Divine Presence.[91] This will lead us to the messianic idea of redemption.

As we hear the final blast of the shofar on Yom Kippur and hasten to prepare for Succot in our days, it is our fervent hope that we may soon hear the blast of the Great Shofar proclaiming that the Messiah has come, the Jewish people have returned to the Torah, they have atoned for their sins and the great succah, the Temple, is about to be rebuilt.

The Midrash[92] explains that the Four Species are signs by which the nations of the world will know that Israel has emerged victoriously from God's judgment, our sins being pardoned. The Four Species themselves atone for the four kinds of death penalty executed by the Bet Din (Court of Law), namely: stoning, burning, death by sword, and strangulation.[93]

The Temple will be Rebuilt

We are told by our Rabbis that of the three pilgrimage festivals, Pesach (Passover) represents the First Temple, Shavuot (Pentecost, Weeks) represents the Second Temple, and Succot (Tabernacles) represents the Third Temple, to be built by the Messiah.[94] Significant events in the Temple's history have always occurred at Succot:

Succot and The Tabernacles of the Wilderness

Even before the Temple there was the Tabernacle (Mishkan), the portable Sanctuary that housed the Holy Ark and the Tablets of Law. After the sin of the golden calf, the Clouds of Glory that had hitherto protected Israel, disappeared. When Moses returned from the mountain with the second set of tablets on Yom Kippur, the Jewish People were commanded to build the Mishkan. The next day he told them to bring donations for the building of the Mishkan which they did for two days. After the materials were gathered together on the 14th Tishri, construction began on the 15th, what would become the first day of Succot. On this day the Clouds of Glory Returned.[95]

---

[91] Rambam, Mishneh Torah, Laws of Repentance 7:6
[92] Midrash: Vayikra Rabbah 30:2, also see 30:7
[93] Weissman M. The Midrash Says: Vayikra, Benai Yakov, New York, 1982, pp333
[94] According to the vision of Ezekial chapters 40-42
[95] Vilna Gaon, according to Rabbi Michoel Schoen, Ohr Somayach, www.virtual.co.il./city_services/holidays/sukkot-8Atzeret/gems.htm

Succot and the First Temple

The dedication of the First Temple of King Solomon at Succot is recorded twice in the Bible:[96]

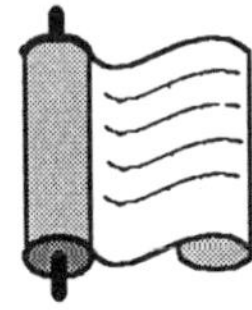

"They gathered before King Solomon - every man of Israel - for the festival [of Succot], in the month of Ethanim,[97] which is the seventh month." (Kings I 8:2)

ויקהלו אל-המלך שלמה כל-איש ישראל בירח האתנים החג הוא החדש השביעי

"On the eighth day they celebrated an assembly, for they celebrated the dedication of the Altar for seven days and the festival [of Succot] for seven days." (Chronicles II 7:9)

ויעשו ביום השמיני עצרת כי חנכת המזבח עשו שבעת ימים והחג שבעת ימים

Succot and the Second Temple

After the return from Babylon, Succot was the first festival celebrated after the building of the Second Temple, recorded by Ezra and Nehemiah:

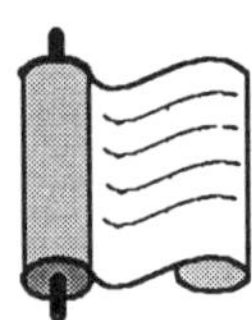

"Then they observed the festival of Succot, as it is written with the burnt offerings of each day in its day according to the [required] amount , according to the law of each day in its day." (Ezra 3:4)

ויעשו את-חג הסכות ככתוב...

The joy of the return from exile and the rebuilding of the Temple gave rise to a celebration of Succot (Nehemiah 8:13,14) unlike anything seen since the time of Joshua:

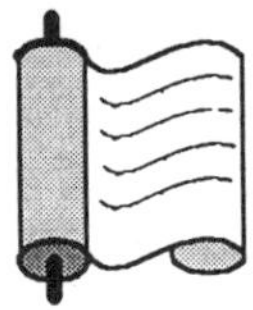

"The entire congregation that had returned from captivity made succot (booths) and dwelt in succot (booths). The Children of Israel had not done so from the days of Joshua son of Nun until that day, and there was very great joy." (Nehemiah 8:17)

ויעשו כל-הקהל השבים מן-השבי סכות וישבו בסכות כי לא-עשו מימי ישוע בן-נון כן בני ישראל עד היום ההוא ותהי שמחה גדולה מאד

[96] This is the section of the prophets (Haftarah) read today on the 2nd day of Succot.

[97] האתנים Meaning "The Strong" or "The Ancients"

Succot and the Third Temple

Just as the first two Temples were dedicated at Succot, may we merit to see the Third Temple dedicated by the Messiah at Succot. Indeed the word succah is sometimes used to refer to the Throne of David and the Temple, begun by David.

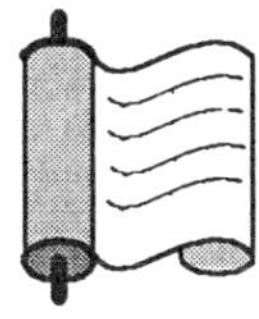

"...on that day I will raise up the fallen booth [succah] of David." (Amos 9:11)

בוים ההוא אקים את-סכת דויד הנפלות

This verse is the basis for an additional verse recited during the grace after meals for Succot:

הרחמן הוא יקים לנו את סכת דויד הנפלת

"The compassionate One! May He erect for us the fallen booth of David."

The Activities of the Temple will be Reinstituted

After the rebuilding of the Temple, the Sanhedrin will be reconstituted, the sacrifices reestablished, and the Jubilee Year declared. Particularly associated with Succot will be the public reading of the Book of Deuteronomy by the King:

"Moses commanded them saying: 'At the end of seven years, at the time of the Sabbatical year, during the Succot Festival, when all Israel comes to appear before Hashem your God at the place that He will choose, you shall read this Torah before all Israel, in their ears. Gather together the people—the men, the women and the small children, and your stranger who is in your cities-so they will hear and so that they will learn, and they shall fear Hashem, your God and be careful to perform all the words of this Torah.' " (Deuteronomy 31:10-12)

The Jewish People will be Redeemed and the Exiles Returned to Israel

According to the Torah, God's "Clouds of Glory" accompanied Israel along their journey through the desert.[98] These clouds protected Israel from

[98] Exodus 14:19,24. Exodus 40:38. See also Babylonian Talmud, Succah 11b, Rashi. According to Rabbi Akiva, the succah represents the actual booths used by the

the heat of the desert sun above, provided a smooth surface for them to cross the rocky desert terrain, and shielded them from the sight and arrows of their enemies.

When we speak about "dwelling in booths" at the time of the Exodus, we are not just referring to the temporary man-made shelters, but to the succah of Hashem, formed by the Clouds of Glory.[99] Thus the building of a succah reminds us of the miraculous protection afforded us by Hashem and His divine mercy. Not only then, but throughout history, if it were not for God's protection of the Jewish people, we would cease to exist. The knowledge of this special relationship with God gives rise to "true joy."

Just as the Clouds of Glory protected us after our redemption from Egypt, so too will God's full protection be restored to the Jewish People at the time of the Final Redemption, at the coming of the Messiah. Under God's protection, the exiles will return to Israel as Isaiah (11:11; 43:5) foretells:

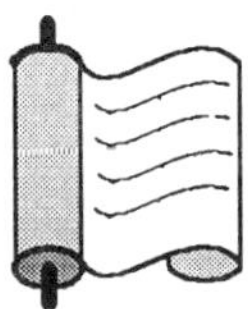

> "There will be a road for the remnant of His people that will remain from Assyria, as there was for Israel on the day it went up from the land of Egypt." (Isaiah 11:16)

The succah of clouds is a picture of the protection that God will bestow upon the Jewish People in the age of the Messiah. It will shield the righteous from the increased intensity of the sun[100] and the storm that will be sent to punish the wicked. Again Isaiah tells us how:

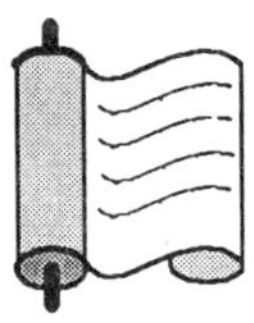

> "And there will be a tabernacle (succah) as a shade from heat in the daytime, as a protection and refuge from storm and from rain." (Isaiah 4:6)
>
> וסכה תהיה לצל-יומם מחרב ולמחסה ולמסתור מזרם וממטר

There will be an Age of Prosperity

Isaiah tells us that in the messianic there will be an abundance of water and therefore an abundance of food, and prosperity:

Children of Israel. According to Rabbi Eliezer, the succah represents the Clouds of Glory.

99 Midrash Tanchuma 22

100 This intense radiation will also heal the sick.

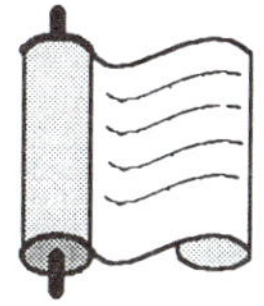

> "...water will have broken out in the wilderness, and streams in the desert." (Isaiah 35:6)[101]
>
> כי-נבקעו במדבר מים ונחלים בערבה

Symbolic of the messianic era, there are many connections between Succot and water:

Water Libations

One of the ways that the Succot[102] offerings differed from those made on other occasions was in the water libations. In the morning[103] three logs (about 1 litre) of water would be collected into a golden flagon from the well of Shiloach[104] just outside Jerusalem and taken in joyous procession where its arrival at the eponymous Water Gate of the Temple courtyard was heralded by a series of shofar blasts. The Cohen (priest) would ascend the ramp of the altar where he would turn to his left to find two silver bowls. Each bowl had a snout that would allow the contents to flow onto the top of the Altar simultaneously, and therefrom through a hole into deep pits[105] beneath it. Since water is less viscous than wine, for the liquids to empty onto the Altar simultaneously, the western bowl for water had a narrower spout than the eastern bowl for wine.

Since the people, both individually and collectively, are judged at Succot in regard to how much water they will receive in the coming year,[106] the

---

[101] Psalm 126:4, relating to the return of Israel to its land, *states "Hashem return our captivity like springs in the desert."* Here the word for springs אפיקים (afikim) refers to the streams formed by flash floods and is a metaphor for the future ingathering of the exiles. Just as water makes a desert bloom, so too will our return from exile gladden our hearts (Rashi). The further connection between water, redemption, and the messianic era is reinforced.

[102] Numbers 29:12-34. Unlike the other offerings, the Torah does not explicitly state that a Water Libation is required. Nonetheless this offering is performed in accordance with the Oral Tradition revealed to Moses and can be deduced from these verses (Babylonian Talmud, Taanit 2b).

[103] Water for the libation to be performed on the Sabbath was collected before the Sabbath and stored in an unconsecrated vessel in a chamber overnight (Tractate Succah: Babylonian Talmud 48a; Mishnah 4:10).

[104] Also translated as Shiloah or Siloam

[105] These "shittin" have existed since creation. The Gemara (Babylonian Talmud, Succah 49a) also records the opinion of Rabbi Eleazar ben Zadok that the wine collected in a cavity below the altar. Once in seventy years the congealed wine would be removed and burned.

[106] Babylonian Talmud: Rosh Hashanah 16a, and Taanit 2a

Water Libation[107] ceremony entreated God to judge the people favorably in this regard. Plentiful water will ensure bountiful crops.

The Water Libation defined by the Oral Law[108] was rejected by the Sadducees. At one time a Sadducee occupied the position of High Priest.[109] Instead of pouring the water over the altar, as prescribed, this dissident poured it over his feet.[110] The worshippers in the Temple, being faithful Pharisees pelted him angrily with their esrogim. The impact of at least one esrog was sufficient to damage the horn of the altar. Josephus,[111] in his *Antiquities,*[112] identifies this Sadducee as the Hasmonean King and High Priest Alexander Yannai (107-76 BCE). In retaliation, 6000 congregants were slaughtered by the king's mercenary and non-Jewish soldiers.

Simchat Bais HaShoaiva[113] *Celebration of Water Drawing*

The drawing of the water from the pool of Shiloach was a joyous event, not only because of the unique water libations, and not only in gratitude towards God for the water of the previous year, but also in celebration of the Oral Law from which the Water Libations are derived.

The verse from Isaiah provided the theme for this "Celebration of Water Drawing " - Simchat Bais HaShoaiva שמחת בית השואבה:

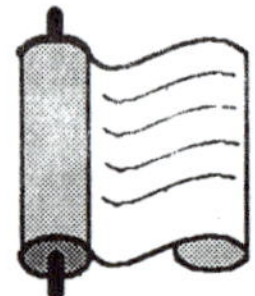

"You can draw water with joy from the springs of salvation" (Isaiah 12:3)

ושאבתם-מים בששון ממעיני הישועה

---

[107] Babylonian Talmud, Succah 48a et seq.

[108] Babylonian Talmud, Taanit 2b. The requirement for a Water Libation is alluded to from variations in the spelling used to define the libations for Succot, described in Numbers 29.

[109] Babylonian Talmud, Succah 48b. Also see Succos, Mesorah Publications, New York, 1995, pp60. Some interpretations (for example see Jewish Encyclopedia, pp261-262) of this event seem to view the account given in the Mishnah (Succah 48b) and its accompanying Gemara as two separate events.

[110] Because of this, the Mishnah (Succah 4:9) records, the congregants would call out to instruct the priest to raise his hand so that they could see where the water was being poured.

[111] According to a footnote in the Soncino Talmud, Succah, p226 (48b)

[112] 13:13:5: Josephus, with an English Translation by Ralph Marcus. Vol VII. Jewish Antiquities, Books XII-XIV, Harvard University Press, Cambridge, 1965, pp413

[113] Literally: Celebration in the House (Place) of Water Drawing

In Temple times, Succot was therefore a time of great excitement and joy. The Talmud declares that *"Whoever did not see the Rejoicing of the Water-Drawing, never saw rejoicing in his life."*[114]

Prior to the beginning of Succot, special balconies were erected in the courtyard to allow women to view the festivities without frivolous intermingling. When the first day of Succot had drawn to an end, tall candelabras, 50 cubits high were erected. Each candelabra had four large reservoirs containing 30 logs (about 10 litres) of oil and were filled by a strong and agile young priest able to climb one of the four ladders[115] The flames were so brilliant that every courtyard in Jerusalem was illuminated and even small objects such as grains could be discerned.

Playing their flutes, cymbals, harps and other instruments, the Levites entered the Outer Court from the Inner Court standing on the fifteen steps corresponding to Psalms 120-134 which begin "A Song of Ascents" (or "Steps").[116] Young and old danced through the night with the Sages performing all manner of feats.[117]

Rabbi Shimon ben Gamliel would juggle up to eight flaming torches or perform a "kidah": Prostrating himself, and supported only by his thumbs, he would kiss the ground and return to an erect position. Rabbi, Levi dislocated his hip attempting this feat, but could juggle eight knives. Samuel could juggle eight glasses of wine without spilling a drop. Abaye, it is said, could juggle eight eggs. Although the Outer Court was small, miraculously it was able to accommodate the thousands of celebrants.

Each morning a prolonged shofar blast announced the start of the procession to the pool of Shiloach, lead by the flute, the loudest of the instruments.[118] Shofar blasts marked different stages in the procession as

---

[114] Babylonian Talmud: Succah 51b

[115] Babylonian Talmud: Succah 51a. Mishnah 5:2-5

[116] These Psalms were composed by King David after the following incident. In preparing for the construction of the Temple, David dug the pits below the Temple (according to the view that they did not exist there from creation - see footnote 105). The waters of the Deep arose and threatened to submerge the world until David cast into the waters a pottery shard onto which had been written the Ineffable Name of God. The waters subsided to such a degree, that with the utterance of the Songs of Ascent, the waters returned to a more modest level (Babylonian Talmud, Succah 53a).

[117] Babylonian Talmud: Succah 51a and 53a

[118] Babylonian Talmud: Succah 50a

the Levites descended the steps, and as they reached the courtyard and the east gate. On the eve of the Sabbath during Succot, additional blasts were sounded when the water was drawn.[119]

Nowadays Simchat Bais HaShoaiva celebrations are held in succot around the world. The fifteen Psalms (120-134) of Ascents are recited recalling the festivities led by the Levites on the fifteen steps between the Inner and Outer Courts. In Jerusalem the streets are filled with dancing and song and prayer that Hashem will speedily rebuild the Temple and with the Messiah, our joy will be even greater than ever it was in days of old.

Four Species and Water

The Talmud teaches us that one of the reasons for the taking of the Four Species is to obtain a favorable judgment concerning rain:

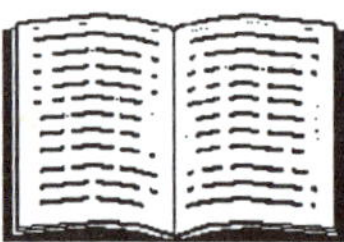

"Rabbi Eliezer said: 'these Four Species serve only to entreat God [to judge us favorably] concerning water. [For by holding them we convey that] just as it is impossible for these Four Species to grow without water, so too, it is impossible for the world to exist without water.' "[120]

Maimonides offers another reason for the Four Species:

"And it seems to me that the four species which comprise the lulav symbolize the joy of their leaving the desert - which was a land devoid of seed, figs, grapes, and pomegranates, with no water to drink -- for a place with fruit-bearing trees and rivers. And in remembrance of this, we take the most beautiful of all fruit and the most pleasantly fragrant, and the most beautiful of all leaves and the best of the grasses -- by which I refer to the willow of the brook."[121]

Just as the Four Species symbolized the joy of entering Israel after the long journey through the desert, so too by taking the Four Species, may we merit to return to Israel after our long exile at the coming of the Messiah.

---

[119] Shofar blasts were sounded for other reasons, see Mishnah Succah 5:5

[120] Babylonian Talmud: Taanit 2b

[121] Rambam, Guide to the Perplexed III:43

Rain, Redemption, and Pardon

A verse in Psalms connects the redemption and pardon of the Jewish people with rain, all of which are concepts associated with Succot and the messianic era:

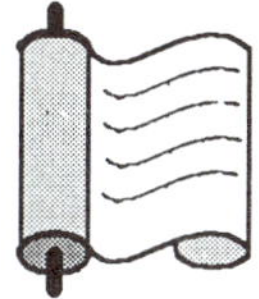

"Hashem: You have favored Your land [with rain], You have returned the captivity of Jacob. You have forgiven the iniquity of Your people." (Psalms 85:2-3)

Reward and Punishment of the Nations

As we have already learned, Zechariah (14:18-19) describes that the punishment for the nations who do not come to the Temple at Succot in the time of the Messiah, will be lack of rain and drought.

Furthermore those many nations will desire to repent and will complain to God that they were not given the opportunity to perform the commandments as were the Jews. God will then judge them by giving them one commandment: to build and dwell in a succah. Even this they will find difficult and reject angrily. God will then explain to them how, in contrast, the Jewish people are willing to immerse their whole bodies and dedicate them to fulfilling God's commandments.[122]

The Nations of the World will Together Worship the One True God

The Book of Kings tells us that on Succot Solomon announced that The Temple would always be open to the gentiles who wished to pray and to proclaim God's Name:

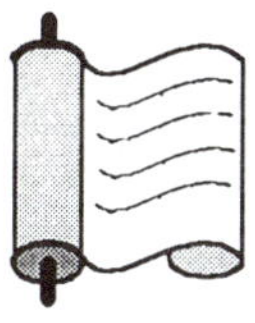

"Also a Gentile who is not of Your people Israel, but will come from a distant land, for Your Name's sake - for they will hear of Your great Name and Your strong hand and Your outstretched arm -- and will come and pray toward this Temple -- may You hear from heaven, the foundation of Your abode, and act according to all that the gentile calls out to You, so that all the peoples of the world may know Your Name, to fear You as [does] Your people Israel, and to know that Your Name is proclaimed upon this Temple that I have built." (Kings 1 8: 41-43)

---

[122] Babylonian Talmud, Avoda Zarah 3, see also Torah Anthology, Me'am Lo'ez. 12:211, Moznaim Publishing, Brooklyn, 1990.

In the events preceding the coming of the Messiah, Gog will come to the land (of Israel), in war, *"in order that the nations may know Me"* (Ezekial 38:16). After the coming of the Messiah, all of mankind will come to worship Hashem and observe His commandments,[123] in peace, at Succot:

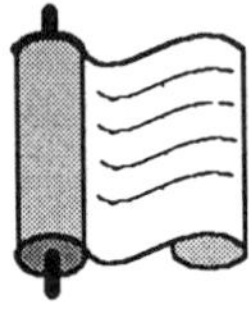

"It shall be that all those who are left over from the nations who had invaded Jerusalem will come up every year to worship the King Hashem, Master of Legions, and to celebrate the festival of Succot." (Zechariah 14:16)

והיה כל-הנותר מכל-הגוים הבאים על ירושלים
ועלו מדי שנה בשנה להשתחות למלך ה"
צבאות ולחג את-חג הסכות

The nations will also come to the Temple on the Sabbath and New Moons:

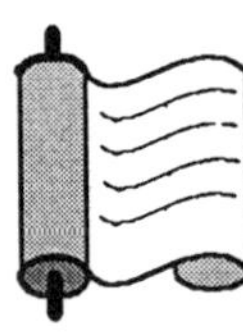

"It shall be that at every New Moon and on every Sabbath all mankind will come to prostrate themselves before Me, says Hashem." (Isaiah 66:23)

והיה מדי-חדש בחדשו ומדי שבת בשבתו יבוא
כל-בשר להשתחות לפני אמר ה"

There will be an Age of Eternal Peace and True Knowledge of God

One of the most salient Jewish teachings about the Messiah is that he will usher in an age of peace and the brotherhood of all man. How do we see this reflected in the Festival of Succot? It is said that the world stands on three pillars (Torah, Avoda, G'milut Chasadim),[124] each of which is represented by one of the three Biblically ordained pilgrimage festivals:

---

[123] This includes the prohibition against idolatry. Most Jewish authorities hold that the personification of God, and the deification of a human being are proscribed by the second of the Ten Commandments. The Trinitarian notion that God can be divided into three parts runs counter to the Jewish concept of His indivisible nature. The opinions that the Trinity represents three aspects of a one God are seen as an attempt to compromise with pagan polytheism.

[124] Mishnah, Avot 1:2

	Torah (Law)	Avoda (Service to God)	G'milut Chasadim (Kindness)
Festival	Shavuot Weeks, Pentecost	Pesach Passover	Succot Tabernacles
Meaning	Giving of the Law	From Egyptian slaves to servants of God	Harmony between fellow men

The creation of the world has purpose, namely the coming of the Messiah, the redemption of the Jewish people and finally an age of peace and universal knowledge of God. Just as the work of the week prepares us for the Shabbat, so too does world history prepare us for the messianic era in which the "canopy" (succah) of peace is established over the Jewish people and the world. The Sabbath then is a taste of the World to Come and so it is appropriate that in one of the Sabbath blessings we refer to God as He

> "Who spreads the canopy (succah) of peace on us and all His people Israel and on Jerusalem."
> הפורש סכת שלום עלינו ועל כל עמו ישראל ועל ירושלים

During the Grace after Meals for the Sabbath we again allude to the messianic era when there will be one long Sabbath:[125]

> "The compassionate One! May He cause us to inherit the day which will be completely a Sabbath and a rest day for eternal life."
> הרחמן הוא ינחילנו יום שכלו שבת ומנוחה לחיי העולמים

The succah, and Succot then are symbols of peace and the breakdown of barriers between humans. In Succot we see harmony among mankind at several levels: within Israel, among all nations, and between the nations and the Jewish people.

Succot: Unity and Harmony within Israel

The leadership Jewish people throughout history has been divided between the tribe of Ephraim-Joseph and the tribe of Judah. When Jacob and his sons went to live in Egypt, the fledgling nation was under the leadership of Joseph. The Jewish people were lead into the Land of Israel by Joshua, of

[125] Based on the Babylonian Talmud: Tamid 7:4

the tribe of Ephraim. The pinnacle of Israel's glory was achieved under King David of the tribe of Judah. This was shattered two generations later when Jeroboam from Ephraim revolted against the Davidic dynasty to form the northern kingdom of Israel, together with nine other tribes. These tribes were scattered and lost when the Assyrians conquered the northern kingdom in 722 BCE.

After the coming of the Messiah, Isaiah and Ezekial both foretell the reunification of the 10 northern tribes of Israel (under Ephraim) with the two southern tribes (represented by Judah):

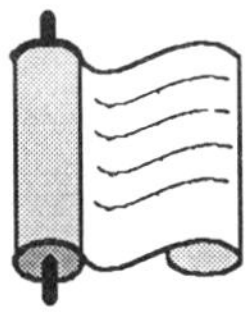

> "Now you, Son of Man, take for yourself one piece of wood and write upon it, 'For Judah and for the Children of Israel, his comrades'; and take one piece of wood and write upon it 'For Joseph, the wood of Ephraim and all the House of Israel, his comrades'. Then bring them close to yourself, one to the other, like one piece of wood, and they will become united in your hand." Ezekial (37:16-17)
>
> "Ephraim will not be jealous of Judah, and Judah will not harass Ephraim." (Isaiah 11:13)

This is not merely a physical reunification of lost brothers, torn apart by the Assyrians. Nor is it a rapprochement between the ten northern tribes led by Ephraim and the two southern tribes led by Judah. This is a spiritual reconciliation of the children of Jacob (Israel), now ready, united, and mature to accomplish its mission in the selfless service of God[126] under the leadership of the Messiah. Ezekial elaborates:

---

[126] The historical rift between Israel (represented by Ephraim-Joseph) and Judah may have its roots in the differences in nature of these two main segments of the Jewish people. Joseph (meaning to "add-on") exemplified learning and self-improvement, while Judah ("to submit") was the epitome of self-sacrifice and self-effacement. At the time of Jeorboam's mutiny, these differences resulted in the unreadiness of the "personal growth" element, (Joseph) to yield to the "servitude" of Judah -- as Judah, centuries earlier, had acknowledged the predominance of "Joseph" in the initial stages of Israel's mission. In other words, Israel had not yet matured to the ultimate realization of its mission selflessly serve God. The resolution of this rift is the key for the ultimate redemption of the Messiah and the perfection of the world in the harmonious service of its Creator. (Anonymous: Chabad Lubavitch in Cyberspace. www.chabad.org)

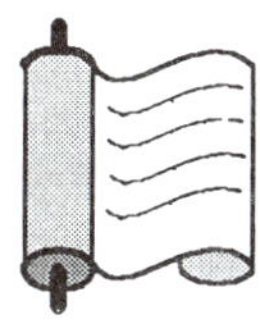

> "I will make them into one nation in the land.....and one king will be a king for them all....My servant David will be a king over them....My servant David will be a leader for them forever." (Ezekial 37:22-25)

How is this unity of the Jewish people reflected in the celebration of Succot? The Torah (Leviticus 23:43) commands us to leave our permanent dwellings and to live in succot, temporary structures, with two, three or four walls. The lack (or non-necessity) for a completed fourth wall allows each family to see into the succah of their neighbors. The flimsy walls and open roofs permit one family to hear the conversation, laughter, and song of the next. In Israel today at Succot whole blocks erupt in unison as one family begins a song of praise, to be joined successively by neighbor after neighbor. In describing Succot, this is what the Torah (Deuteronomy 16:15) must mean to *"be completely joyous"* והיית אך שמח

The idea of unity among the Jewish people is also inherent in the taking of the Four Species, representing each type of Jew. In this interpretation,[127] each of the Four Species represents one of four kinds of Jew who comprise the Jewish people:

- The Esrog (citron: smell and taste) is the Jew who combines Torah study with good deeds.
- The Lulav (date palm: taste but no smell) is the Jew who studies Torah, but does no good deeds.
- The Hadas (myrtle: smell but no taste) is the Jew who performs good deeds, but does not study Torah.
- The Arava (willow: no smell, no taste) is the Jew who neither studies Torah nor performs good deeds.

According to this Midrash, God said, *"I do not want to destroy even the last group; let all four groups unite so that one can atone for other."* In both interpretations the esrog has a special place. As the "heart," if a perfectly beautiful esrog is held close to the three other species (other parts of the body), they too will be elevated by the person's refined emotions and actions. Similarly by placing the "esrog" Jew, close to the "lulav," "hadas" and "arava" Jews, all of Israel will endure and become elevated.[128]

---

[127] Midrash: Vayikra Rabbah 30:12

[128] The taking of the Four Species can also be symbolic of the unity of the Jewish people. On this theme there is the question of the reunification of the ten Lost Tribes, whose identity has been the subject of speculation for centuries. According to some theories the Native Americans may be one of the lost tribes. It is therefore

According to another interpretation, each of the Four Species symbolizes unity and harmony: *"The Esrog remains on the tree from year to year so that the young and old dwell together."*[129]

Other interpretations of the Four Species[130] relate to figures in Jewish history worthy of emulation. The three hadasim (myrtle branches) refer to the three patriarchs, the two aravot (willow branches) refer to Moses and Aaron, the lulav refers to Joseph and the esrog to King David. These are all the "Ushpizin" the guests that we invite into the succah on each of the seven days. By uniting the Four Species (representing the seven leaders of the Jewish people) we are uniting our people through the ages. By inviting them into the succah we are in a sense enacting the resurrection of the dead under the eternal "Canopy of Peace" (i.e. the succah) that will mark the messianic era.

The idea of harmony and unity is expressed in the special assembly of Israel when the king reads publicly from the book of Deuteronomy:

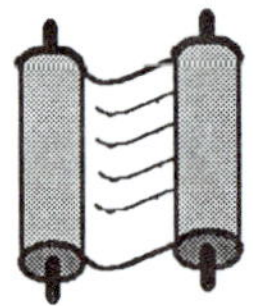

> "At the end of seven years, at the time of the Sabbatical year, during the חג הסכות Succot festival, when all Israel comes to appear before Hashem your God, in the place that He will choose, you shall read this Torah before all Israel, in their ears." (Deuteronomy 31:10-11)

Succot: Unity and Harmony among Nations

The idea of all nations coming to know the name of Hashem, and coming to Jerusalem to worship at Succot has already been mentioned (Zechariah

---

noteworthy that there is a tribe in Tennessee, related to the Seminole Tribe of Florida, that sits in booths every autumn, performing a religious ceremony with palm fronds and citrus fruit (In: Wein, B: "Fall of the Northern Empire," Jewish History Lectures, Yeshiva Shaarei Torah, Suffern, New York, 1987). There is some speculation also that because of many similarities in Shinto ritual, the Japanese are believed to be descended from one of the Ten Lost Tribes. A particularly festive event in the Japanese calendar is Obon, predating the introduction of Buddhism and celebrated originally on the 15th day of the 7th (lunar) month. Another interesting custom is the use of a plant branch in sanctification ceremonies. From: Israelites Came To Ancient Japan, Arimasa Kubo, www.ask.ne.jp/~remnant/isracame.htm

129 Siddur of the Baal Ha-Tanya (R' Shneur Zalman of Liadi, founder of the Chabad-Lubavitch movement), cited by Stern, pp44.

130 Midrash: Vayikra Rabbah 30:10, also Succos, Mesorah Publications, New York, pp58

14:16). Those with even a superficial appreciation of the history of the Middle East and its center stage in world history will immediately realize that this could not be possible without the unity and harmony among all the nations of the Earth that will follow the Messiah. Thus, Succot comes to represent the basic unity of all human beings. This will be a time of complete rejoicing for all those within Israel:

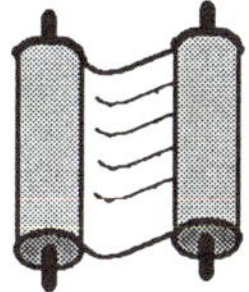

> "You shall make the חג הסכות festival of Succot for a seven day period, when you gather in from your threshing floor and from your wine cellar. You shall rejoice on your festival – you, your son, your daughter, your slave, your maidservant, the Levite, the proselyte,[131] the orphan, and the widow who are in your cities. A seven day period shall you celebrate to Hashem, your God in the place that Hashem, your God will choose, for Hashem will have blessed you in all your crop and in all your handiwork, and you will be completely joyous והיית אך שמח" (Deuteronomy 16:13-17)

Succot: Unity and Harmony between the Nations and Israel

We have already seen the uniqueness of Succot among all the festivals of the Torah and its ramifications for the nations of the world. Nowadays, Jerusalem is filled with Gentiles during Succot. *"It is as if their heartstrings are pulled by some invisible magnet, the source of which they know not. Some force draws them to connect between Succot and the location of the Holy Temple."*[132]

The importance of the Temple and of Succot for the redemption of the Gentiles is clear from Solomon's proclamation (that the Temple will be open to Gentiles)[133] and Zechariah's prophesy (that the nations will worship in Jerusalem).[134] In Temple times sacrifices were (and will be)

---

[131] Note that the word גר, which the ArtScroll Tanach translates as "proselyte," may also be translated as "resident alien," one who is not Jewish, but who accepts upon himself the Seven Laws of Noah. The word גר may also be translated to mean "convert."

[132] "The Festival of Sukkot (Tabernacles)" Rabbi Chaim Richman, The Restoration Newsletter, September, 1996 (Tishri, 5757)

[133] *"so that all the peoples of the world may know Your Name."* Kings 1: 41-43

[134] *"It shall be that all those who are left over from the nations who have invaded Jerusalem will come up every year to worship the King Hashem, Master of Legions, and to celebrate the festival of Succot."* Zechariah 14:16

brought on behalf of the nations to atone for their sins,[135] to invoke Heavenly protection for them, and to pray for peace and harmony between them. Starting with 13 bulls on the first day of Succot, and diminishing to 7 on the seventh day (Numbers 29:12-33), a total of 70 sacrifices represent the 70 Gentile nations descended from Noah (Genesis 10:1-32).

Sadly, the Midrash relates,[136]

> "...if the nations of the world had only known how much they needed the Temple, they would have surrounded it with armed fortresses to protect it for it was greater value for them than for Israel."

Today, in place of these sacrifices we recite the appropriate passages from the Book of Numbers that describe the Seventy Sacrifices for the Nations.

Feast of the Leviathan

After the coming of the Messiah the Righteous will be sheltered by a specially constructed succah as foretold by Isaiah (4:6):

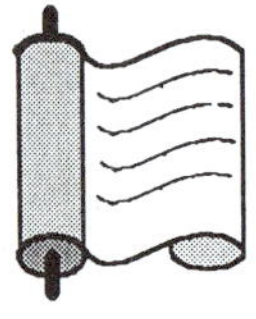

> "And there will be a tabernacle (succah) as a shade from heat in the daytime, as a protection and refuge from storm and from rain." (Isaiah 4:6)
>
> וסכה תהיה לצל-יומם מחרב ולמחסה ולמסתור מזרם וממטר

According to the Talmud this succah will be constructed from the skin of the Leviathan,[137] a giant fish created on the fifth day of Creation. In these succot, the Righteous will eat the delicious meat of the Leviathan and the Behemoth,[138] a huge ox-like creature created on the sixth day of Creation.

---

[135] Babylonian Talmud: Succah 55b

[136] Midrash Bamidbar Rabbah 1,3. Rabbi Yehoshua Ben Levi

[137] Babylonian Talmud, Bava Basra 75a. It is not clear whether the descriptions of the Leviathan and Behemoth should be taken literally or allegorically on a Kabbalistic level. The Lubavitcher Rebbe explains how the feast of the Leviathan signifies the revelation of the rationale underlying the Torah and the commandments (Likkutei Sichos, XV, p. 420).

[138] Babylonian Talmud, Bava Basra 74b: Pesachim 119b

After the Messiah has come, God will give the Leviathan and Behemoth the signal to fight. They will kill each other: the Behemoth with the sharp fin of the Leviathan, and the Leviathan with the horns of the Behemoth.[139]

In recognition of this special succah, as we leave the succah for the last time each year we make the following declaration:

> "May it be Your will, Hashem, our God and the God of our forefathers, that just as I have fulfilled the mitzvah and dwelled in this succah, so may I merit in the coming year to dwell in the succah of the skin of the Leviathan. Next year in Jerusalem."

As at the conclusion of the Passover Seder, we leave the succah with the same hope for the messianic era:

> Next year in Jerusalem
> לשנה הבאה בירושלים

Final Judgment and Resuscitation of the Dead: Hoshana Rabbah

That the month of Tishri is a time for judgment is exemplified by its *mazal* (zodiac sign) which is *moznayim* (Libra-scale).[140]

The Messianic elements of Hoshana Rabbah are clear: salvation, return, the Messiah, prosperity (rain) and the resuscitation of the dead. Although we are judged on Rosh Hashanah, and our verdict sealed on Yom Kippur, the sentence is not ratified until Hoshana Rabbah. The intervening time in a sense is a time for appeal. Engaged in the mitzvot (commandments) of Succot we are actually making our final efforts of repentance and appealing before the Final Judgment on Hashanah Rabbah.[141] So too in the messianic age when our final judgment will be on Hashanah Rabbah, the Righteous will be revived. On this day the souls of the Righteous with be at one with Hashem, residing under His throne and delighting in the radiance of the Divine Presence.

---

[139] Midrash: Leviticus Rabbah 13:3

[140] A discussion of Kabbalah, the Jewish mystical tradition, is beyond the scope of this book. The "signs of the zodiac" have kabbalistic significance which bears little resemblance to the popular "astrology" of the secular world. If, when, how and by whom this knowledge is to be used is strictly determined by Jewish Law.

[141] Some have noted the significance of the coincidence of Hoshana Rabbah 5707 (October 16 1946) with the execution of the Nazi war criminals.

It is also on this day that the number of bulls sacrificed on behalf of the nations (Numbers 29:12-33) diminished from 13 (on the first day of Succot) to 7, making a total of 70, representing the Nations descended from Noah. Why are the sacrifices for the nations arranged in this descending order, and not equally arranged with 10 per day, or in ascending order, starting with 7 and ending with 13?[142] The answer is that throughout Succot we are representing the decline in the power of the nations that oppose God's will. Just as Jericho (representing the stronghold of Caananite idolatry) was destroyed by six daily circuits followed by seven circuits on the seventh day, so to will the evil nations be destroyed at the Final Judgment on Hoshana Rabbah. This will leave those who will fulfill the purpose for which humanity was created, under the earthly reign of the Messiah son of David, in turn under the Heavenly reign of Hashem.

It is not surprising therefore, that on Hoshana Rabbah the seventh of the Ushpizin is David, prototype of the Messiah and representative of the Sephira (attribute with which God interacts with creation) of Kingship (see Ushpizin - Exalted Guests, page 25).

Will Gentiles have a Share in the World to Come?

An often asked question is "Is it necessary for Gentiles to convert to Judaism to enter the World to Come?" The answer is no. Our sacred literature declares that the Chasidei Umot Haolam (Pious Ones of the Nations) have a blessed share in the World to Come. Such people[143] ("Noachides", or "Children of Noah") are those who uphold the Seven Laws of Noah. These are in fact seven categories of laws deduced from Genesis 9:1-17 by the Talmud.[144]

These laws must be upheld not because they are logical laws, but rather for the reason that they are God's will, and for no other reason. The reward for keeping the commandments given by God to humankind (both Jew and

---

[142] There is a general principle that we ascend in holiness, rather than descend. This is why we light one more candle each day of Chanukah, rather than the same or a diminishing number.

[143] A number of examples are given in Jewish literature. The Babylonian Talmud (Taanit 29a) describes the case of a Roman official who saved Rabban Gamliel from execution and who entered the "World to Come."

[144] Babylonian Talmud: Sanhedrin 56a (pages 56-60); Rambam, Hilchos Melachim 9:1. See also Rabbi Aaron Lichtenstein ("The Seven Laws of Noah", www.noahide.com/lawslist.shtml) who, based on Maimonides, defines the 66 Noachide Laws that make up the seven categories. Rav Shmuel ben Hophni Gaon defines 30 Noachide Laws.

non-Jew) is a share in the World to Come consisting of a intense closeness to God. Our punishment for their violation is remoteness from God. God balances the accounts of our deeds and renders judgment about our position in the World to Come. How He does this is beyond our comprehension, but we trust that He is just and merciful.

The Seven Noachide Laws - The Seven Laws of the Children of Noah[145]

1. The prohibition of idolatry[146]
2. The prohibition of blasphemy
3. The prohibition of murder
4. The prohibition of theft
5. The prohibition of sexual immorality
6. The requirement to establish Courts of Law and a system of justice
7. The prohibition of cruelty to animals

These laws must be upheld not because they are logical laws, but rather for the reason that they are God's will, and for no other reason. The reward for keeping the commandments given by God to humankind (both Jew and non-Jew) is a share in the World to Come consisting of a intense closeness to God. Our punishment for their violation is remoteness from God. God balances the accounts of our deeds and renders judgment about our position in the World to Come. How He does this is beyond our comprehension, but we trust that He is just and merciful.

Just as a Jew is rewarded for keeping the 613 commandments of the Torah, and punished for violating them, a non-Jew is rewarded or punished with regard to the Seven Laws of Noah. S/he is not punished for violating the laws incumbent on a Jew. Although Judaism accepts sincere converts, it takes great pains to discourage them. This is because a Noachide only has seven commandments to transgress and therefore seven ways to lose his/her share in the World to Come. A Jew has 613 such opportunities. Thus allowing someone to convert disadvantages them if they are do not fully understand the implications of violating all the laws incumbent on a Jew. However there is great reward for someone who

[145] There are some opinions that the giving of charity is a commandment to the Children of Noah, while others say that this is not a commandment, but is nonetheless meritorious. There is also an oral tradition that the Children of Noah are forbidden to interbreed animals of different species or to graft trees of different kinds (The Path Of The Righteous Gentile, Clorfene C and Rogalsky Y, Feldheim, NY, 1991) also at www.chabad.org/gopher/outlook/7laws/

[146] See footnote 123

understands, accepts and is prepared voluntarily to discharge these responsibilities.

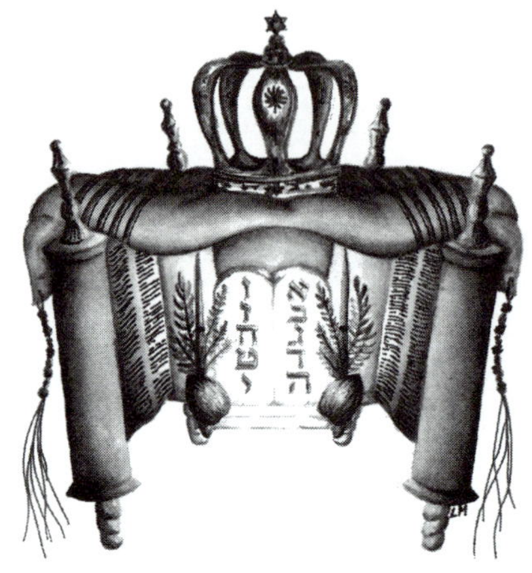

Eph. 2:8-9 Only!

Balanced by Titus 3:5-8!

CHAPTER 6: THE MESSIAH? WHO AND WHEN?[147]

Who Will He Be?

The Messiah will be a descendent from King David who will be both scholarly and righteous. He will be a leader capable of leading us to final military as well as spiritual victory. Almost to the level of Moses, he will have perfected himself in word and deed.

In the symbolism of the Four Species the esrog represents not only the Jew who studies and observes the commandments of the Torah, but also it represents King David. The fusion of the two ideas leads us to the Messiah, a descendent of David, who will be perfect in words and deeds and who will lead us to our eventual redemption and a time of peace.

Above all, the Messiah will be a human being. According to Maimonides,[148] *"one should not entertain the notion that the King Mashiach must work miracles and wonders, bring about new phenomena within the world, resurrect the dead, or perform other similar deeds."*

Messiah, Son of Joseph

There are a number of references in Jewish sources to the warrior "Messiah, ben[149] Joseph" (i.e. from the Tribe of Joseph) who will die in a great battle (in the War of Gog and Magog) to reliberate Jerusalem.[150] The death of this individual will move Israel to the grief described in Zechariah 12:12, and will precipitate the arrival of the Messiah ben David, who will lead us to full redemption. The Messiah ben Joseph is also alluded to as one of the Four Craftsmen (Messiah Son of David, Messiah Son of Joseph, Elijah and Shem) who will bring the Jews to their land.[151]

The Messiah from the tribe of Joseph (Ephraim), as the messianic representative of the Northern Kingdom is the embodiment of the

---

[147] See footnote 82 for primary sources.

[148] Rambam, Hilchos Melachim 11:3

[149] Ben = son of

[150] Jerusalem will be liberated from the Roman Armilus (seen by Christians as the "anti-Christ"), according to Saadia Gaon the Egyptian born Jewish sage, 892-942 CE, cited by Sarachek p43

[151] Zechariah 2:3, Babylonian Talmud, Succah 52b

messianic prophecy of the unification of Israel.[152] Indeed it is noteworthy that the connection between Messiah ben Joseph, and the messianic aspect of Succot may be alluded to by the correspondence of the month of Tishri (in which Rosh Hashanah, Yom Kippur and Succot fall) and the Tribe of Ephraim. Each of the twelve months corresponds to one of the Twelve Tribes. Tishri begins the autumn season (tekufah), whose three months correspond to the three tribes of the camp of Ephraim - Ephraim, Menashe, Benjamin - who were situated to the west in the desert encampment.[153]

It should be noted that the concept and role of the Messiah ben Joseph is not universally discussed or understood[154] as well as the concept of the Messiah ben David. Strictly speaking he is a personage of the "pre-messianic" age. Indeed Maimonides chooses to remain silent on this matter in his discussion of the Messiah. Furthermore, according to the Zohar,[155] the Heavenly decree concerning the death of Messiah ben Joseph has been nullified.

Some Christian writers have attempted to equate the Messiah ben Joseph with the "first" coming of their messiah. According to this argument, the "first" coming is as the suffering servant. The "second" coming is as the conquering king. The interpretation belies a confusion of the meaning of words used in Biblical and modern literature. The term "messiah" means an "anointed one", or a leader of people[156] Thus the Messiah ben Joseph and Messiah ben David are two leaders, in this case of the Jewish people. Contrastingly, the Christian term "Messiah" means a divine person in whom belief will bring about atonement or salvation.

In a curious reversal, Abrabanel[157] describes the appropriation by some Christians of the Messiah ben Joseph as "Anti-Christ." This long-awaited Jewish redeemer would, they feel, come to frustrate the messiahship of their redeemer, who had already come. Thus it was important to discredit this Jewish messiah by developing the concept of an anti-messiah.

---

[152] It is not claimed that this individual will lead the ingathering of the 10 Lost Tribes.

[153] Rabbi Yitzchak Ginsburgh, Gal Einai, www.virtual.co.il./city_services/holidays/sukkot-8Atzeret/gal.htm

[154] For a secular, academic discussion of the Messiah ben Joseph see: Klausner J. The Messianic Idea in Israel. Macmillan, New York, 1955, Chapter IX

[155] Cited in note #1 to Babylonian Talmud, Succah 52a, ArtScroll edition

[156] This can apply to a leader of any people - Cyrus, King of Persia was also referred to as a "messiah" (see Isaiah 45:1).

[157] Isaac Abrabranel, the great sage, Jewish Statesman and leader of the Spanish Jewish community at the time of the Spanish expulsion, cited by Sarachek, p263

How will we recognize the Messiah, Son of David?

According to Maimonides we will consider, but not affirm him as Messiah if:[158]

- He is from the House of David[159]
- He is a Torah scholar
- He observes the precepts of the Written and Oral Law
- He compels Israel to observe the Law and repairs the breaches in its observance
- He fights the wars of God

Only when he has succeeded in the above, builds the Temple and gathers the dispersed remnant of the Jewish people, can he be declared the Messiah. At this point he will perfect the entire world motivating all the nations to serve God together:

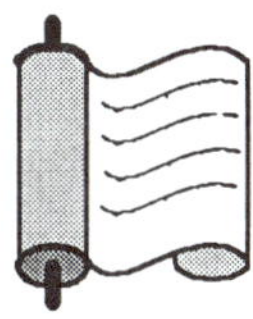

> "I will change the nations to speak a pure language, so that they all will proclaim the Name of Hashem, to worship Him with a united resolve." (Zephaniah 3:9)
>
> כי-אז אהפך אל-עמים שפה ברורה לקרא
> כלם בשם ה" לעבדו שכם אחד

When will he come?

The Talmud[160] states that the world will last 6000 years.[161] With each year corresponding to a day,[162] these 6000 years correspond to the days of Creation, with the Sabbath day as the messianic age.[163] The first two thousand years, approximately to the time of Abraham,[164] were the years of void. The next 2000 years, from Abraham to the destruction of the Second

---

[158] Mishneh Torah, Hilchos Melachim 11:4

[159] Specifically through Solomon, and also not through Jeconiah. See Appendix 3: Biblical Depiction of the Messianic Age, page 98

[160] Babylonian Talmud, Avoda Zarah 9a. For an extensive discussion of the timing of the messianic era, see also Babylonian Talmud, Sanhedrin, Chapter 11.

[161] The Hebrew Calendar is reckoned from the creation of Adam, the first man with a soul. 1999 CE is equivalent to 5759 in the Hebrew Calendar.

[162] Babylonian Talmud, Sanhedrin 97a & b, citing Psalms 90:4: *"For even a thousand years in Your eyes are but a bygone yesterday"*

[163] Many Christians also believe the messianic age will begin 6000 years after creation. This is derived directly from Jewish sources, partly from their interpretation of Jewish sources, and partly from Christian sources. See Good, p51.

[164] This is the approximately time that Abraham destroyed the idols of his father and departed for Canaan (Jewish Timeline Encyclopedia Kantor, M. Aronson, Northvale, NJ, 1992).

Temple were the years in which Torah flourished and the last 2000 years are the "Days of the Messiah," the time when it is possible for the Messiah to come, only after the destruction of the two Temples.[165]

There are various scenarios which will precipitate the coming of the Messiah. If the Jewish people so merit by their repentance he will come immediately. He may also come in the event of an impending disaster to the Jewish people, or if they degenerate into heresy.[166] The Talmud further explains that in the period immediately preceding the Messiah insolence will increase, honor will dwindle and there will be no rebuke.[167]

Jacob attempted to reveal the time of the Messiah to his sons but his prophetic knowledge was removed from him before he could do so.[168] Daniel alluded to the End of Days (7:25; 12:7) but was commanded to conceal the calculations that were revealed to him (Daniel 12:4). These are hints to us that we should occupy ourselves with the Torah in the present world. Maimonides summarizes this well:

> "...neither the sequence of these events nor their precise details are among the fundamental principles of the faith. One should not occupy himself at length with...these and similar matters, nor should he deem them of prime importance, for they bring one to neither the awe nor the love [of God]. Similarly, one should not try to calculate the appointed time [for the coming of Mashiach]. Our Sages declared:[169] "May the spirits of those who attempt to calculate the final time [of Mashiach's coming] expire!" Rather, one should await [his coming] and believe in the general conception of the matter." Maimonides[170]

---

[165] Babylonian Talmud, Sanhedrin 97a, citing Hosea 6:2. *"He will heal us after two days, on the third day He will raise us up and we will live before Him,"* where the two days refer to the Two Temples, and the third day refers to the Third Temple.

[166] Babylonian Talmud, Sanhedrin 97b

[167] Babylonian Talmud, Sanhedrin 97a. In other words, governments will be so corrupt that they cannot be called to account.

[168] Genesis 49:1; Midrash Genesis Rabbah 98:2; Babylonian Talmud, Pesachim 56a

[169] Babylonian Talmud, Sanhedrin 97b

[170] Rambam, Hilchos Melachim 12:2

CHAPTER 7: SUCCOT IN CHRISTIAN THEOLOGY

It is somewhat surprising to learn that Christianity, a faith based on the belief of a savior, has not adopted or adapted Succot, a festival steeped with messianic associations. Although through the ages there have been Christians who have observed Saturday as the Sabbath as well as other Jewish holidays, this phenomenon has gained popularity more recently. In particular, a number of churches and individuals have started to believe and understand that Succot has some meaning for their faith.

What are some of the ways that Christians have begun to understand Succot in the context of their beliefs?[171]

Succot: Main Themes of Christian Understanding

For mainstream Christians there is much significance to Succot.[172] The early Jewish Church kept the festivals of Judaism and incorporated the concept that the festivals found their fulfillment in Jesus, whom they regarded as the Messiah. This concept shaped both theology and worship practices within the early Jewish Church, and Hebraic custom and tradition was passed to Gentile congregations as well. For most Christians today the Biblical Festivals are a shadow of things to come, revealing God's redemptive plan through their messiah (Colossians 2:16-17).

In Christian theology, the three pilgrim festivals of Judaism, also mirror the Triune Godhead:

- Pesach/Passover emphasizes the victory of the Son of God over sin and death, as the work of atonement, and the ratification of a new covenant, which was completed at this festival.
- Shavuot/Pentecost emphasizes the work and person of the Holy Spirit, who was poured out on the day of Shavuot/Pentecost. This outpouring signifies that the "last days" have begun, as Joel's prophecy has been

[171] In writing this section I am fully aware that the views presented here include those of minor denominations within the Church. Some of these ideas have been expressed by people who describe themselves as "Jewish" but who believe that Jesus of Nazareth is the Messiah. Since this is the cornerstone of the Christian faith I have therefore included these views in this section.

[172] I am deeply grateful to Charity Dell who has provided much of this introductory material.

fulfilled, and God's "servants and handmaidens" now cooperate in spreading the good news to the ends of the earth.

- Succot/Tabernacles emphasizes the Father who lives in and with His people. God's tent is now with redeemed humans who have been through tribulation and have overcome evil through *"the blood of the lamb and the word of their testimony"* (Revelation 12:10-12).

The strongest tie early Jewish and Gentile Christians felt to Succot grew out of the teachings of Jesus during Succot, as recorded in the seventh chapter of John. Although the Book of John was penned in Greek, its imagery, themes and structure are rooted in Hebraic patterns and theology. John emphasizes the teachings of Jesus at several Jewish festivals, including Pesach (Chapter 13), Succot (Chapter 7) and Chanukah (10:22).

Christian theology views the seventh chapter of John as pivotal: Firstly, Succot is seen as a precursor to the promised outpouring of the Holy Spirit (Joel 2:28--32), later realized on Shavuot/Pentecost (Acts 4). Secondly, Succot is the shadow of that which is to come, the time when God finally "tabernacles" with His people in the new heavens and new earth. (Revelation 21:1-4)[173] Although Christian theology sees the Kingdom of God as being present (for believers), Succot is the festival when this Kingdom will achieve its ultimate fulfillment at the consummation of human history, as depicted in the Book of Revelation.

Other Aspects of Succot Observance

There are millions of Christians who seek to emulate the founder of their faith, to learn about Judaism, and to express solidarity with the Jewish people. In some cases it is out of respect for God's promise to Abraham:

"I will bless those who bless you, and him who curses you I will curse." (Genesis 12:3)

ואברכה מברכיך ומקללך אאר

In other cases it is a means to evangelize Jews or because their particular theology allows for some co-existence of Judaism and Christianity.[174] At a fundamental level, there is the feeling that since Succot will be the time of

---

173 Indeed the ideas expressed by Revelation 21:3, taken in isolation, capture the essence of the Jewish scriptures.

174 Hagee

the Messiah, and that if Christians are to participate in the events of that time, they must begin to understand Succot and to incorporate it into their established ritual.

Instructing the Disciples to Celebrate Succot, and the "Second Coming" at Succot

Jesus' instruction to his disciples to celebrate Succot in Jerusalem (John 7:2-6) is seen as an instruction for all time. Just as his disciples celebrated Succot, so too should his believers celebrate it in the future. The refusal of Jesus to *"show himself to the world"* (John 7:4-6) at that particular Succot because his *"time has not yet come"* (John 7:6) is seen as an allusion to his "second coming" at the Succot of the future.

Succot = Christmas ??

We have already mentioned the existence of pagan festivities at the time of the winter solstice and the desire of the early church to "Christianize" these days. A number of Christians[175] have deduced from the Christian Bible that Jesus could not have been born in December, but was in fact born in late September, on the first day of Succot.[176]

Because of the influx of pilgrims into Jerusalem for Succot, they argue, Joseph and Mary were forced to seek accommodation in Bethlehem. Furthermore, according to the thesis,[177] the "wise men" from the east were sages who were making the pilgrimage from Babylonia, the main Jewish community outside of Israel at that time. The "tidings of joy" reflected one of the names for Succot, "The Season of our Joy," and the star that they saw, they saw through the roof of their succah. In citing Genesis 33:17, where Jacob builds shelters (Succot) for his animals, also the place of Jesus' birth, the thesis is complete.[178] This then would have also placed the date of his circumcision, on the eighth day after birth, namely Shemini Atzeret, the Eighth day of Solemn Assembly.

---

175 Hagee p191; Treybig et al., p8; Chumney p178, Killian: http://24.130.12.78/greg/succoth.html. See Rosh HaShanah and the Messianic Kingdom to Come, Joseph Good, 1989, Hatikva Ministries: www.hatikva.org/birth.html

176 See Appendix 6 for full details of this calculation.

177 The Mishnah, Avot 5:7, however states in regard to the Pilgrimage Festivals that no man ever said *"There is insufficient space for me to stay in Jerusalem."* All pilgrims were sufficiently accommodated.

178 To extend the thesis, the calculated date of conception would have been 25th Kislev, the first day of Chanukah. Thus, one Christian remarked, the so-called "light of the world," was conceived on the festival of lights (Chanukah)!

The Esrog - Citron - and Christian Theology

It is hardly surprising that a Jewish symbol as powerful as the esrog would be incorporated into Christian Theology.

In its simplest form the feminine symbolism of the esrog is linked to Mary, the mother of the founder of Christianity. In a more convoluted series of equations based on verses in the Song of Songs, the mother is likened to the Cedar of Lebanon. Since the citron was considered by some to be a variety of cedar, or in fact was the cedar, we are thus left with an association, albeit one based on false premise, between the immaculate purity of the esrog and that claimed by some for the mother of Christianity. Oranges and lemons have at times been substituted for the citron and individually or severally, the citron, orange and lemon serve as the basis for other Christian legends surrounding its founder, which in turn are depicted in the religious art of Renaissance Italy.[179]

Other associations, tenuous though they may be, might be derived if one is allowed to consider a Christian assertion that the Tree of Life of the Garden of Eden represents in some way their savior, and a Jewish tradition that the Tree of Knowledge of Good and Evil was in fact the esrog tree; even if we are speaking of two different trees. Based on a Midrashic interpretations of the esrog as King David (and hence the Messiah),[180] the association with the Christian messiah is easy to make.

A more recent writer equates the esrog with the non-Jewish believers of the Christian messiah who will be *"gathered in."*[181]

The Lulav - Palm Branch - in Christian Theology

When Jesus rode into Jerusalem six days before Passover, he was greeted with palm branches (John 12:13). By using palms, the disciples were, perhaps, making a connection between Jesus and Succot, and therefore with Jesus as the Messiah.

---

[179] Tolkowsky, pp177 et seq. A clear example of this is the depiction of by Girolamo de Libri (1474-1551) "Madonna, child and Saint Anne" seated in front of a citron tree replete with fruit and blossom. (Plate LXIV). At the time of Tolkowsky's work, this painting was in the National Gallery in London.

[180] Midrash: Vayikra Rabbah 30:10, also Weissman, 1982, pp332, also Succos, Mesorah, pp58

[181] Chumney, p168, 169, no source cited

"On the next day much people that were come to the feast, when they heard that Jesus was coming to Jerusalem, took branches of palm trees, and went forth to meet him, and cried Hosanna: Blessed is the king of Israel that comes in the name of the Lord (John 12:12-13).

The greetings are taken directly from Psalm 118 which is part of the Hallel (see page 30) recited on the three Pilgrimage Festivals and on New Moons:

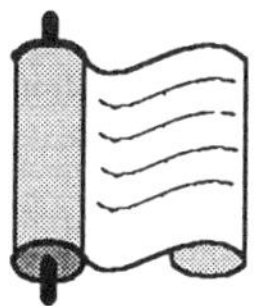

"Please Hashem, save now! Please Hashem, bring success now! Blessed is he who comes in the name of Hashem. (Psalm 118:25-26)

Accordingly it is Church custom to recite this Psalm for both Palm Sunday, the start of Holy Week, and Easter Day.

I have often supposed, but I have yet to find a source for it, that the orb and scepter,[182] the symbols of royalty, have some relationship to the esrog and lulav respectively. I have recently found that the lulav has been called the "Palm of Martyrdom." In a work by the Italian artist Pietro da Cortona (1596-1669), the baby Jesus is depicted as giving what is clearly a lulav (the central unopened palm frond) to a woman, Saint Martina.[183]

Christian Adaptations of other Jewish Messianic Motifs of Succot

Since the messianic significance of Succot was undoubtedly known in the first century CE, the fact that Jesus even dared to preach during Succot (John 7:14) is seen by Christians as an indication of his messiahship.[184] A number of aspects of Succot have also been said to represent Jesus:

- the succah is seen as Jesus, providing a covering for his believers[185]

---

[182] These are not uniquely Christian symbols, but the Orb of Christian monarchs has a cross in the place of the pitam of the esrog.

[183] Madonna and Child with Saint Martina. The work is held by the Kimball Art Museum, Fort Worth, Texas. The work's caption states that the child is giving the palm (of martyrdom) to Saint Martina, martyred for her refusal to pray to pagan gods. It is unclear from the picture who is giving and who is receiving the palm.

[184] Glaser and Glaser, p181.

[185] Revelation 21:3; Chumney p162 (citing Hebrews 9:11) also Chumney, p172; no source cited

- the tremendous illumination of Jerusalem during the celebration of the Water Drawing Ceremony is Jesus as *"the light of the world"* (John 8:12; 9:5)[186]
- and the flute,[187] being a "pierced" instrument, represents the *"pierced"*[188] Jesus

In the Book of John, Christians learn that the "living water" (of the Water Libation) was in fact, their messiah (as Holy Spirit) and that this was the water that would flow out of the innermost being of each person (i.e. believers) filled with it:[189]

> "In the last day, that great day of the feast[190], Jesus stood and cried, saying, 'If any man thirst let him come unto me, and drink. He that believes on me, as the scripture has said, out of his belly shall flow rivers of living water.' " (John 7:37-38)[191]

The famous verse from Isaiah sung during the Water Drawing Ceremony: *"You can draw water with joy from the springs of salvation."* (Isaiah 12:3) is taken as an allusion to Jesus given the similarity of the word ישועה (salvation) with the Hebrew word for Jesus - ישוע.[192] The pouring of the wine and the water on the altar in the water libation of Succot is further seen as the blood and water that Jesus is said to have shed on the cross.

The succah, as the Clouds of Glory, is also seen as the believers in Jesus.[193] The temporary nature of the succah is regarded as the temporary nature of Jesus' *"first dwelling among men"*[194] and the joy (simcha) of Succot (Season of our Joy) has been linked to the "tidings of great joy" described in Luke (2:10). Finally, the ingathering of the harvest is seen as the ingathering of the believers in Jesus.

---

[186] Glaser and Glaser, p184

[187] The Babylonian Talmud, Succah 50a, describes its featuring role in the procession of the Water Drawing Ceremony.

[188] The term "pierced" is often used to refer to Jesus: John 19:34; Revelation 1:7

[189] Charity Dell, Glaser and Glaser p179.

[190] There is a debate among Christian writers as to whether this speech took place on Hoshana Rabbah or Shemini Atzeret. Glaser and Glaser p177.

[191] See also John 4:14, and Chumney p184

[192] Chumney p171

[193] Chumney p157, citing Hebrews 12:1 and Revelations 1:7.

[194] Chumney p159, citing John 1:14

We have seen (Succot: Unity and Harmony within Israel, page 59) how, in the Torah, the Messiah will reunify the northern (represented by Ephraim) and the southern (represented by Judah) kingdoms split apart by the Assyrians in 722 BCE (Ezekial 37:16-17; Isaiah 11:13). Some Christian writers have equated this to a reconciliation of Jews (Judah) and Gentiles (Ephraim). The switching (crossing) of Jacob's hands when blessing Ephraim and Menashe (Genesis 48:14) signifies the cross, Ephraim is taken to represent Christianity. A similar allusion is taken from the derivation of the name "Ephraim," meaning "fruitful" (Genesis 41:52) since the believers in Jesus as messiah are said to be "exceedingly fruitful."[195]

Quite what the nature of this reconciliation is believed to be, is unclear: perhaps it is the incontrovertible revelation to the Jews of the truth of Christian assertions, or the harmonious co-existence of the two faiths.[196]

According to one Christian enactment of this latter alternative, this reconciliation is seen as that of the prodigal (Luke 15:11-32) son (Ephraim/ early Christianity) with his older brother (Judah/ the Jewish People) who kept the Torah. Citing Hosea, the messiah will come when both Judah and Ephraim acknowledge a certain guilt:

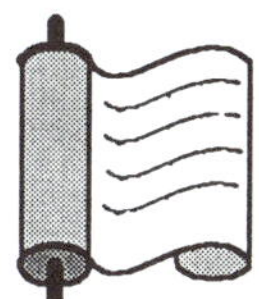

> "I wil go, I will return to My place until they will acknowledge their guilt and seek My face" (Hosea 5:15)
>
> אלך אשובה אל-מקומי עד אשר-יאשמו ובקשו פני

The guilt of Judah, is seen as the Jews' non-acceptance of the Christian messiah. The guilt of Ephraim is the adoption of Roman paganism and anti-Semitism and the departure from the Torah and the faith of their savior. Here the comparison between the perversion of Christianity and that of Ephraim (the Northern Kingdom) is rather explicit and possibly shocking to many mainstream Christians:[197]

---

195 See Chumney: "Ephraim is a prophetic picture of the bride of Christ": www.hebroots.org/

196 See also Hagee. In Mormon theology this reunification represents a unification of the Torah (Stick of Judah) with the Book of Mormon (Ephraim). See www.jewsforjudaism.org/nojavasite/webdocs/ Mormons/sticks.htm

197 Chumney: "Ephraim is a prophetic picture of the bride of Christ": www.hebroots.org/

- Just as Ephraim forsook the Torah (Hosea 8:12), so too did Christianity.
- Just as Ephraim substituted Dan and Bethel as places of worship for Jerusalem (Kings I 12:30), so too did Christianity substitute the church for the synagogue.
- Just as Ephraim substituted holidays rather than observing the dates and times of the Biblical festivals (Kings I 12:32),[198] Christianity has adopted Christmas and Easter from Roman Mythryism.[199]
- Just as Ephraim instituted a substitute priesthood (Kings I 12:31),[200] Christianity allows pastors and priests to be ministers who are not anointed and called by God into their office.
- Just as Ephraim introduced idol worship (Kings I 12:32)[201] and called it the true worship of the God of Israel, so too has Christianity mixed Roman and Babylonian practices and beliefs with the true worship of the God of Israel and called it the true worship of the God of Israel.

Accordingly,[202] Christianity was punished with the dark ages and until it repents from these sins, Jesus cannot return. When will this occur? According to this thesis, and with a day representing 1000 years[203] the answer of 2000 years is given by Hosea:

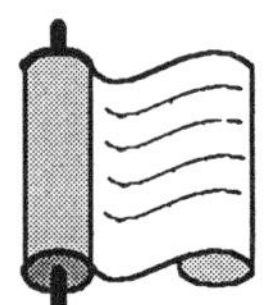

"He will heal us after two days, on the third day He will raise us up and we will live before Him." (Hosea 6:2)

יחינו מימים ביום השלישי יקמנו ונחיה לפניו

Christian Observance of Tabernacles

Christian celebration of Succot views Succot as the celebration of: the autumnal harvest in the natural world, the reenactment of Jesus' celebration of this festival and the consummation of the Kingdom of God, to be realized at the end of time. These ideas have found expression in a variety of ways:

---

[198] As defined in Leviticus 23. Jeroboam instituted a holiday one month after Succot, in imitation of the true Succot.

[199] See footnote 207

[200] These priests were not from the Tribe of Levi

[201] Jeroboam instituted the worship of calves.

[202] Chumney citing Hosea 5:3 et seq: "Ephraim is a prophetic picture of the bride of Christ": www.hebroots.org/

[203] Psalms 90:4: *"For even a thousand years in Your eyes are but a bygone yesterday."*

Sabbath-Observing Churches

A number of churches have evolved which seek to return to the Hebrew roots of their faith. Many believe that the Divinely ordained Biblical Feasts are to be upheld by all nations and are a shadow of things to come revealing God's redemptive plan through their messiah (Colossians 2:16-17).[204] In adopting Jewish practices many of these "messianic" or "Sabbath-Observing"[205] Christians believe that just as a naturalized alien has all the rights and responsibilities of a native citizen, so too have they been inserted into the Sinaiatic Covenant, as depicted in Romans:

> "and so if some of the branches [of the live tree] be broken off, and you being a wild olive tree, were grafted in among them, and with them partake of the root and fatness of the olive tree" (Romans 11:17)

The olive tree here represents the Nation of Israel, and the wild olive tree represents (Sabbath-Observing) Christian believers.[206] Although Romans 11 is discussed widely in Christian writings it seems that those who call themselves "Sabbath-Observing" understand this to mean that only by upholding the Laws of the Torah will they receive the benefits of grafting.

Attempting to uphold the Judaic faith of the early Church, many of these Christians have shunned Christmas[207] and Easter[208] and refrain from

---

[204] See Treybig et al., 1999, who also discuss the pagan origins of Christmas, Easter, and Halloween. Also see Glaser and Glaser.

[205] Not to be confused with the Church movement that seeks to evangelize Jews.

[206] I am grateful for Dean Wheelock for his insight on this point. See Hebrew Roots 96-1, page 4. Hebrew Roots, Lakewood, Wisconsin.

[207] Pagan festivals abounded at the time of the winter solstice, with common themes running through the practices of the Babylonians, Egyptians, Greeks, and Romans, as well as ancient Druid, German and Celtic tribes. Often celebrating the "resurrection" or return of slain or departed deities, these festivals incorporated trees (fir, palm, mistletoe, Yule logs, holly) to represent the gods themselves, the mothers of the gods, fertility, and sexual reproduction. Christmas was first established as a feast in the fourth century and in the fifth century the western Church decreed that its celebration be on the day of the old Roman (Mythryst) feast of the birth of Sol - the sun god.

[208] Although, according to Christian teaching, the events regarding the crucifixion of Jesus were said to have occurred at the time of Passover, the Church nonetheless wished to avoid any coincidence with the Jewish festival and therefore established rules where this would not occur. Furthermore Easter was celebrated at the time of the feast of Ashtoreth (Ishtar, pronounced Easter: see 1 Kings 11:5; 2 Kings 23:13) the queen of heaven whose symbols of fecundity and sexuality included rabbits, eggs, and the lily. Others (Charity Dell, personal

wearing crosses or other well known Christian symbols, because of their pagan associations.[209] Instead they observe Saturday as the Sabbath[210] and uphold many other Jewish laws such as the abstaining from pork and shellfish. Some eat only fish that have fins and scales and purchase only kosher food.[211] They may not observe these precepts according to the Shulchan Aruch,[212] but for these Christians,[213] the Jewish calendar is their calendar, Jewish law is their law, and Judaism is their religion, except of course for the belief in the founder of their faith as the incarnation of God and their savior.[214]

Alternative to Halloween

At one level Christian celebration of Succot has occurred as a reaction to the increasingly violent nature of Halloween. What used to be enjoyed by many American children as a time of happy "trick-or-treating" has evolved into a time of apprehension and fear. Every year incidents are reported in which children are severely injured by a "treat" that contains poison or a razor blade. The preceding "mischief" night has provided an excuse for some to engage in acts of vandalism, looting, and burning. Parents and church leaders have begun to recognize the pagan nature of Halloween and are attempting to provide safe and non-pagan alternatives.

---

communication) have suggested that Easter is entirely derived from Passover and that the association of "Easter" with pagan gods is the result of confusion between similar sounding names.

[209] At the Council of Nicea (325 CE) the anti-Semitic Constantine outlawed circumcision, and replaced Passover with Easter, and Shabbat with Sunday. The early Catholic Church also "Christianized" the pagan Saturnalia by establishing Christmas.

[210] Again the day of the Sabbath was changed to Sunday by the Church for fear that Judaization would take place: *"Christians shall not Judaize and be idle on Saturday, the Sabbath, but shall work on that day; but the Lord's day (Sunday) they shall honor, and as being Christians, shall, if possible, do no work on that day. If, however, they are found Judaizing, they shall be shut out from Christ."* - Canon 29, Council of Laodicea, 364 CE
"All things whatsoever it was the duty to do on the Sabbath, these we have transferred to the Lord's day (Sunday)... because it is more honorable than the Jewish Sabbath." - Eusebius of Caesarea, 4th century (from Killian)

[211] Fins and scales are the signs of a kosher fish defined by the dietary laws in Leviticus 11). Although most do not eat meat slaughtered according to Jewish law, these churches buy meat from sources known to drain the blood well from the animal, as their equivalent to Jewish practice.

[212] Codification of Jewish Law, compiled by Rabbi Joseph Caro in the 16th Century

[213] Some individuals do not apply the term "Christians" to describe themselves, and are even offended by the term. They see themselves as Orthodox Jews in every sense, except for the belief in Jesus as the messiah.

[214] For examples of this see: "The Watchman" http://members.aol.com/gkilli/home/ and also "Hebraic Roots of Christianity Global Network" www.hebroots.org/

As a child attending secular school in England I remember a "Harvest Festival" where food was collected and given to the poor. As a Jew it was obvious that this had its origins in Succot. As an Englishman it seems that Thanksgiving is derived from this "Harvest Festival." Many churches have revived the idea of a harvest or fall festival, which they celebrate on October 31st, Halloween, with games, crafts, prayer and Bible study.[215]

Seeking a meaningful experience of this festival in a way that is more than a just reaction to pagan practice, some churches have realized that the Jewish founder of their faith celebrated a harvest festival known as Succot. As one devout Christian proudly exclaimed: *"If it was good enough for Jesus, it is good enough for me."* We have the curious phenomenon of Succot being celebrated on October 31st some two to six weeks after the date of the Jewish thanksgiving, and about three weeks before the American one!

Examples of Christian Celebration of Tabernacles

Christian celebration of Tabernacles borrows many ideas from Jewish observance. The building of the succah and other festival preparations are times of family and community togetherness. From a Jewish perspective, there is no requirement for Gentiles to uphold these festivals given to Israel in the Sinaiatic Covenant. This is also a view held by many churches, but for the reason that the Christian teachings represent a "new covenant" obsoleting the "old".

An independent, interdenominational evangelical church in Dallas, Texas, builds a large (over 100' x 50') succah in its grounds and covers it with palm branches. It holds prayer and Bible study sessions in the succah throughout the seven days of the festival and encourages families to eat in it. The Church also uses the Four Species and believes that all the Biblically described festivals should be practiced by Christians, including Purim, and Chanukah, which is alluded to in the Christian Bible (John 10:22).

A Fellowship Church in Colorado also builds a succah every year and holds services for three days corresponding to the first three days of Succot. Normally this church holds its services to coincide with the Jewish celebration. One pastor told me that in the year that Succot was held a week too early *"the celebration just did not feel the same."*

---

[215] See Halloween Alternatives, L. Merryman, Winepress Publishing, Mukilteo, WA, 1996.

A Pentecostal church in New Jersey, holds their Tabernacles service as a non-pagan, Biblically-based alternative to Halloween. The service integrates Hebraic and African-American worship traditions. The church is decorated in fall colors with a Fall - Harvest Festival motif. After benedictions are said in Hebrew and English, there are scriptural teachings, the Four Species are waved and taken in procession around the indoor succah. There is a reenactment of the Water Drawing Ceremony. Selections of Klezmer,[216] Middle Eastern as well as black gospel music provide the background for much joyful singing and dancing, chassidic dancing being a particular favorite. Congregants wear either tallisim[217] or a T-shirt from Zaide Reuven's Esrog Farm.[218] Bags of nuts and candies are distributed to all who. Dancing and feasting continue after the formal part of the festivities have been concluded.

Of the diverse group of churches described as "Sabbath-Observing" (see Sabbath-Observing Churches, page 81) many observe the other Biblically ordained festivals. Most do so according the accepted Jewish calendar, although some do not "postpone"[219] or accept the authority of Jews to fix the calendar.[220] Rather than build succot, these churches plan communal gatherings at large hotels which serve as "temporary dwellings" for one week. Some church leaders encourage their congregation to save 10% of their income and use it to cover their accommodation, food and

[216] Klezmer is the music of Eastern European Jewry.

[217] Plural of Tallis: A prayer shawl. This four cornered garment resembles those worn in ancient times. In fulfillment of the commandment (Numbers 15:37-41), Tzizit (fringes) are placed on each corner as a reminder to keep all the commandments of the Torah.

[218] We are not aware of any Biblical commandment to wear such a garment.

[219] In order to avert the occurrence of Yom Kippur on Friday or Sunday (so that there are not two consecutive days when food cannot be prepared, or other labors performed which are permitted on a Festival but not the Sabbath or Yom Kippur), and occurrence of Hoshana Rabbah on Sabbath (when the custom of Arava would not be permitted, and the seven Hakafot - processional circuits - performed), Rosh Hashanah is not permitted to fall on a Sunday, Wednesday or Friday. Instead it is "postponed" by one day. There are some circumstances where it is postponed by two days. (Bushwick, N. Understanding the Jewish Calendar, Moznaim Publishing, New York, 1989).

[220] Some groups have split on this issue and have devised complex alternatives to the accepted Jewish calendar. Consequently their observance of the festival may differ by as much as a month. This is reviewed by Norman Edwards: Biblical Calendar Basics, www.best.com/~oasis7/sn/docs/calbas.htm

entertainment expenses at one of these Tabernacles gathering.[221] The first and eighth days are observed as Holy Days with prayer and Bible study sessions, sometimes with joyous dancing and singing. The intermediate days have a lesser degree of sanctity and communal or family recreational activities are planned. Many of these churches do not take the Four Species, but may use one set for teaching purposes.

[221] This corresponds to the "Second Tithe" (Maaser Sheni) of Deuteronomy14:22, which was eaten in Jerusalem on the first, second, fourth and fifth years of the Shmitta or Seven-Year Agricultural cycle, at the time of the three Pilgrimage festivals (Passover, Pentecost and Tabernacles). In the third and sixth year, this tithe (Maaser Ani) was given to the poor (Deuteronomy 14:28).

CHAPTER 8: GOD'S PURPOSE FOR JUDAISM AND CHRISTIANITY

Our Jewish faith is firmly founded in the holy Hebrew scriptures. Directed by Divine decree, we conduct our daily lives and anticipate the End of Days as foretold by our Prophets. Accordingly, we have remained unmoved in our belief that Hashem will send the Messiah who will lead us to redemption, gather us from exile, rebuild the Temple and usher in the age of peace. We have remained steadfast in our belief in the One God, the truth of His Torah, the purpose He has ordained for us and the protection He has afforded us. Through Roman persecution, the Spanish Inquisition, the indignities of Arab rule, the Russian pogroms, the numerous blood libels and expulsions, and the Nazi Holocaust,[222] these beliefs sustained our forefathers. Can our belief be shaken now that we have emerged from the Holocaust, have our own state and are returning to our land?

We are witnessing many remarkable events. The creation of a State of Israel,[223] the building of the land, the return of exiles from Ethiopia and Russia and the building of yeshivot.[224] Jews are returning in large numbers to the faith of their fathers. Within the Christian community we see support for the Jewish people and for Israel,[225] we see apologies and acts of contrition for the wrongs committed by the Church to the Jews,[226] and we see churches abandoning many pagan practices and celebrating Jewish festivals such as Succot. We see the flourishing of congregations of B'Nai Noach, gentiles who observe the Noachide creed, and even the voluntary conversion of entire churches to Judaism. What are we to make of these times and how are we to explain nearly 2000 years of oppression under the Church?

---

[222] Sadly these injustices have not been eradicated. At the time of writing 13 Iranian Jews are imprisoned without trial, falsely accused of spying for Israel and the United States. Also a number of synagogues were burned in San Francisco, and Jews shot at in Chicago and San Francisco, by white "supremacists".

[223] Blech (p327) cites modern Kabbalists who have noted that the verse (Deuteronomy 30:3) which promises that Israel will be returned to its land is the 5708th verse of the Torah. The number 5708 corresponds to the year (1948) in which the State of Israel was founded.

[224] Schools of religious study

[225] Hagee

[226] Hagee, Chumney

God's purpose for Judaism - a Christian View

A number of Christians have attempted to answer this question. According to one Christian minister,[227] Jesus' identity as the Messiah was deliberately withheld from the Jews, so that they would reject him. This would then cause his message to be spread to nations who would never have learned of God. According to this thesis, it is not necessary for Jews to believe in Jesus, since when he does come, God will reveal the truth to the Jews, who will live side by side with the believers in Jesus, grafted into the blessed nation of Israel.

According to some[228] this blindness is mentioned by the book of Romans:

> "...that blindness in part is happened to Israel until the fullness of the Gentiles be come in...(Romans 11:25-27)

In Acts (2:1-4) Pentecost is pinpointed as the time when Jews and other non-Christians will receive the truth of Christianity. With these sources in mind, Joseph Good argues that the Six Day War of 1967, which immediately preceded Shavuot (Pentecost) was the time of the *"fullness of the Gentiles"*, evidenced by the subsequent conversion of more Jews (over 100,000 in the USA) than in the 1900 years since the beginning of Christianity, a trend that he expects to accelerate.

God's purpose for Christianity - a Jewish View

We have seen how some Christians understand the continued existence of Judaism in the context of their faith. As Jews how can we understand the existence of Christianity in the context of our own belief? Maimonides, the great codifier of Jewish Law, has provided us with an answer.[229]

He does so in two parts. Maimonides begins by summarizing the main reasons why Jews do not embrace Christianity. This leads him to formulate his question which he answers in his conclusion.

---

[227] Hagee

[228] Good, p149

[229] From a (Christian) censored passage of Rambam, Hilchos Melachim, 11:4. Sichos In English The Laws Concerning Mashiach: See www.chabad.org/rmbm1112.htm and also www.j4j.addr.com/nojavasite/webdocs/messiah.html. This passage was censored from most editions published since the Venice edition of 1574.

Maimonides: Perspective on Christianity: Introduction

It will surprise most readers (both Jewish and Christian) that Maimonides finds a reference in the Jewish Bible to Jesus!

"Jesus of Nazareth who aspired to be the Messiah and was executed by the court was also spoken of in Daniel's prophecies"[230]

Maimonides cites the following verse:

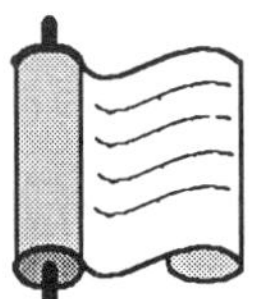

"the sons of the lawless men of your people will exalt themselves to establish a vision, but they will stumble." (Daniel 11:14)

ובני פריצי עמך ינשאו להעמיד חזון ונכשלו

and summarizes the Jewish position:

"Can there be a greater stumbling block than [Christianity]? All the prophets spoke of Messiah as the redeemer of Israel and their savior, who would gather their dispersed ones and strengthen their [observance of] the mitzvot. In contrast [the founder of Christianity] caused the Jews[231] to be slain by the sword, their remnants to be scattered and humiliated, the Torah to be altered, and the majority of the world to err and serve a god other than the Lord."

Maimonides: Why Christianity?

This summation is unequivocal, and the unstated question about God's purpose for Christianity is obvious:

If Christianity is antithetical to Torah, why does God permit it to flourish?

Of course, Maimonides declares, our mortal minds cannot understand God or His Universal plan, but we do accept that it is just:

[230] See also Rashi

[231] To Sabbath-Observing Christians, the slaughter of Jews in the name of Christianity is equally repugnant. This repugnance is intensified considering the likelihood that "Sabbath-Observing" Christians were also slaughtered as heretics and Judaizers. To them, the religion of the Crusaders bears little resemblance to the faith of the early Church, a faith which these Sabbath-Observers attempt to emulate.

Nevertheless, the intent of the Creator of the world is not within the power of man to comprehend, for *"the ways of men are not His ways, nor their thoughts His thoughts"* (Isaiah 55:8, paraphrase)

Having declared his trust in God, Maimonides provides his answer: that Christianity[232] is a vehicles for the dissemination of the universal knowledge of God:

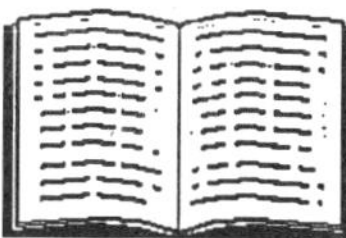

[Ultimately,] all the deeds of Jesus of Nazareth...will only serve to pave the way for the coming of Messiah and for the improvement of the entire world, [motivating the nations] to serve God together, as it is written, *"I will make the peoples pure of speech so that they will all call upon the Name of God and serve Him with one purpose"* (Zephaniah 3:9)

Maimonides elaborates that through Christian evangelism, an otherwise ignorant and totally pagan world will be enlightened about the existence of the One Creator and of His holy Torah:

How will this come about? The entire world has already become filled with talk of [the supposed] Messiah, as well as of the Torah and the mitzvot. These matters have been spread among many spiritually insensitive nations, who discuss these matters as well as the mitzvot of the Torah. Some of them [i.e. the Christians] say: "These commandments were true, but are not in force in the present age; they are not applicable for all time."

Thus, Maimonides concludes, when the Messiah arrives, the Christian (and Islamic) world will have the ability to recognize him and to act accordingly.

---

232 Maimonides makes a similar argument regarding Islam, although one must be careful to distinguish Christian and Islamic beliefs.

CHAPTER 9: WHEN THE MESSIAH FEASTS WITH JEWS & GENTILES

We have seen how the Festival of Succot occupies a central position in the minds of the Jewish People and our yearnings for the Messiah. Steeped in messianic associations, from the Divine Protection of the succah, to the symbolism of the Four Species and the Water Libations, the nexus of Succot and an age of peace and prosperity for the Jewish People is clear.

The Torah tells us also that the messianic age will be for the Righteous of all Nations to enjoy, but provides little detail as to how this will occur. In discussing God's purpose for Christianity and Islam, our great sage Maimonides teaches us that through these religions, the otherwise pagan Nations of the World will be able to recognize the King Messiah, when he arises. They will then accept and worship the One God.

> When the true Messiah king will arise and prove successful, his [position becoming] exalted and uplifted, they will all return and realize that their ancestors endowed them with a false heritage; their prophets and ancestors cause them to err."[233]

This will happen at Succot, the culmination of world history and of God's plan for the present world, in fulfillment of Zechariah's prophesy:

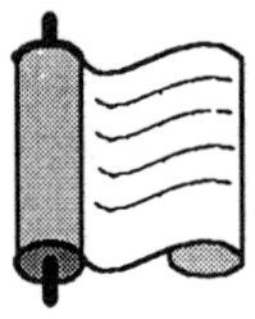

> "It shall be that all those who are left over from the nations who had invaded Jerusalem will come up every year to worship the King Hashem, Master of Legions, and to celebrate the festival of Succot" (Zechariah 14:16).
>
> והיה כל-הנותר מכל-הגוים הבאים על ירושלים
> ועלו מדי שנה בשנה להשתחות למלך ה"
> צבאות ולחג את-חג הסכות

Our eternal hope for the Messiah is captured in the 12th stanza of the Yigdal:[234]

---

[233] Rambam, Hilchos Melachim, Chapter 11

[234] A poetic recreation of Maimonides' 13 Principles of Faith

ישלח לקץ הימין משיחנו לפדות מחכי קץ ישועתו
"By the End of Days, He will send our Messiah to redeem those longing for salvation."

and in the zemer, the song of praise, recited at the conclusion of the Sabbath:

אליהו הנביא....במהרה יבוא אלינו עם משיח בן דוד
"Elijah the prophet May he quickly come to us with Messiah, son of David"

May we go from strength to strength in our observance of the mitzvot of Succot and may we merit to see the coming of the Messiah, speedily and in our days.

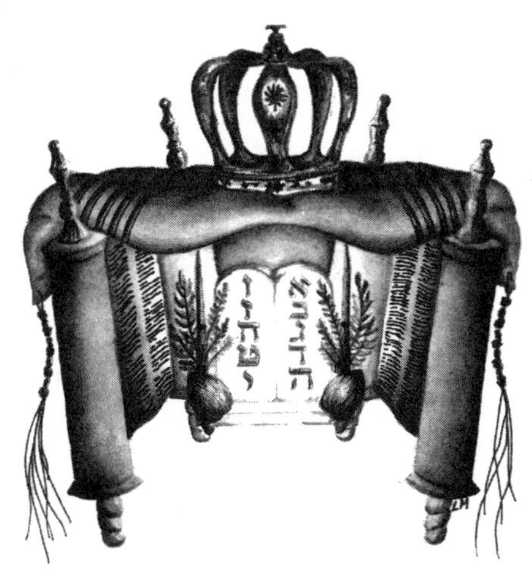

APPENDIX 1: GLOSSARY

Arava	see Four Species
Arba Minim	see Four Species
Av	see Months
Bensch	The Grace (blessings) after Meals
Bet Din	Court of Law
Bracha	Blessing or benediction
Chol Hamoed	The intervening days of Pesach and Succot. The first and last days of these festivals are observed fully with almost all the laws of the Sabbath applying. On the intervening days, certain of the laws do not apply. Nonetheless these days do retain the festive character of the holiday and so matzo is eaten on Pesach, lulav and esrog are taken, and the succah is lived in on Succot. Also special prayers are recited during these days.
Ellul	see Months
Esrog	see Four Species
Four Species	The Four Species, ארבעה מינים, comprising the lulav (palm branch), etrog (esrog, citron), hadas (myrtle) and arava (willow). The Four Species are taken on Succot (see Leviticus 23:40).
Gemara	see Talmud
Hadas	see Four Species
Hakafa (Hakafot)	The celebratory procession made around the synagogue during Succot (except on the Sabbath). Seven Hakafot are made on Hoshana Rabbah.
Halacha	Jewish Law
Hallel	"Praise". Consisting mainly of Psalms 113-118, Hallel is recited on Pesach (Passover), Shavuot (Pentecost), Succot (Tabernacles), and Chanukah. These joyous Psalms speak of five basic aspects of Jewish faith: The Exodus, Parting of the Red Sea, Giving of the Torah, the Revival of the Dead and the Coming of the Messiah. An abridged version of Hallel is sung on the last six days of Passover and on the New Moon (Rosh Chodesh).
Hashem	God. The Four letter name of God is never pronounced, nor is it written, except in holy objects such as prayer books, Torah scrolls and the like. Instead the appellation "Hashem" is used, literally "The Name."
Hoshana Rabbah	The "Great Hoshana," the seventh day of Succot
Kabbalah	The Jewish mystical tradition
Kaddish	Meaning "sanctification," a prayer written in Aramaic, sanctifying the Name of God. The honor of reciting this is given to mourners, who, by its recitation, will increase the merits of their departed relatives during the period of their judgment following death. The prayer is erroneously called "the prayer for the dead," but mentions neither death nor the name of the departed.
Kiddush	Meaning "Sanctification." The blessing or set of blessings said over wine which sanctify the Festival.
Kislev	see Months

koishekal	Holder for the lulav, hadas and arava made from palm leaves.
Kosher	Ritually fit according to Jewish Law. This can be applied to food, ritual objects, witnesses, or procedures.
Lulav	see Four Species
Maariv	The evening prayer said after sundown
Machzor (im)	A special adaptation of the Siddur (daily prayer book) made for each festival. It usually contains all the readings from the Bible as well as the unique order of prayers said on those occasions.
Maimonides	see Rambam
Mashiach	Hebrew for Messiah, meaning "the anointed one."
Midrash	Collections of homiletics, parables and moral legends based on the Bible. Part of the Oral Tradition.
Minchah	The afternoon prayer said before sundown
Minyan	A quorum of 10 Jewish men over the age of 13 required to conduct certain parts of prayer services, including the reading from a Torah scroll, and the recitation of Kaddish.
Mishnah	see Talmud
Mitzvah	A commandment from the Torah
Months	The months of the Hebrew calendar are lunar, starting at the New Moon. For the purposes of counting the months, the first month of the year is Nissan, in the spring time. For the purposes of counting years, the first month is Tishri. The months are in order: Nissan, Iyar, Sivan, Tammuz, Av, Ellul, Tishri, Cheshvan, Tevet, Shevat, Adar. Because of the discrepancy between 12 lunar months and the solar years, a "leap month" of Adar II is intercalated seven times in a cycle of 19 years.
Musaf	The additional prayer said on Sabbaths, Festivals and New Moons. It is recited immediately following the morning prayer, Shacharit.
Pitam	The protuberance on the apex of an esrog. If the pitam remains on the esrog at the time of picking, its later removal renders the esrog invalid for ritual use.
Piyut (Piyutim)	Liturgical poems inserted into the prayer service of festivals which capture the essence of the festival
Rabbi	One who is qualified to render opinions and interpretation of Jewish Law
Rambam	Maimonides, 1135-1204. A great Jewish (Rabbi Moses ben Maimon) scholar who lived in Spain and Egypt, and was physician to the Sultan. Rambam codified Jewish law by subject matter into the famous Mishneh Torah.
Rebbe	A Rabbi of great stature, often with many followers and students
Rosh Hashanah	Jewish New Year
Schul	Synagogue
Shacharit	The morning prayer
Shofar	Horn of a ram or other kosher animal (except cow) sounded at Rosh Hashanah and Yom Kippur
Siddur	Daily prayer book (from the word Seder, meaning "order")
Succah	Booth, temporary structure made on Succot
Succot, Succos	The festival of Tabernacles
Tallis	A prayer shawl. This four cornered garment resembles those worn in ancient times. In fulfillment of the commandment in Numbers

	(15:37-41), Tzizit (fringes) are placed on each corner as a reminder to keep all the commandments of the Torah.
Tanach	The Jewish Bible, comprising: Torah (Pentateuch), Neviim (Prophets), Chetuvim (Writings) - TaNaCh. See Appendix 2
Talmud	The compendium of the Oral Law, transmitted orally since the time of Moses. It consists of the Mishnah (codified around 180CE), previously transmitted orally and the Gemara, further elucidation of the Mishnah. The Babylonian Talmud, compiled in 450CE includes the elucidation (Gemara) of the Jewish sages of Babylon. The Jerusalem Talmud, is less complete and authoritative, and was finished in about 340CE.
Tefillin	Phylacteries. Leather cubes which contain passages written on parchment from the Torah affixed to the arm and head by means of leather straps.

Tefillin

	These are a sign of Israel's holiness and a memorial of the Departure from Egypt. Tefillin are worn in fulfillment of the verse *"And you shall bind them as a sign on your arms and as a frontlet between your eyes"* (Deuteronomy 6: 4-9). Both cubes contain this passage in addition to others which repeat this commandment: (Deuteronomy 11: 13-20; Exodus 13: 1-10; Exodus 13; 11-16). In the cube for the arm these passages are written on one piece of parchment. In the cube for the head, they are written on four separate scrolls, each placed in its own compartment.
Tishri	see Months
Torah	Generally this refers to the entire corpus of Jewish Law, including the books of the Jewish Bible, its commentaries, Midrashim, and the Talmud and its commentaries. More narrowly defined, Torah refers to the Jewish Bible, or just the Five Books of Moses, contained on a Torah Scroll.
Yiddish	The language spoken by Jews of Eastern European descent, it is based on old German with additional words from Hebrew, Russian, Polish and other European languages. Yiddish is written in Hebrew script.
Yom Kippur	Day of Atonement
Zaide	Yiddish for grandfather

APPENDIX 2: A SUMMARY OF THE JEWISH BIBLE AND AUTHORATIVE SOURCES

Torah

The term Torah, usually translated to mean "Law" can be used narrowly or widely. In its narrowest sense "Torah" refers to the Five Books of Moses, or Pentateuch. This is written on a Torah scroll. In a wider sense "Torah" refers to the Jewish Bible, the 24 books of Tanach (see below). In its widest sense "Torah" refers to the entire corpus of Jewish Law and its commentaries.

The additional books of the Christian Bible do not form part of Jewish Scripture. Furthermore, Christian translations of the Jewish Bible must be read carefully since they have often come through Greek or Latin without the benefit of a translator's knowledge of the Hebrew idiom.

The Written Law

The Jewish Bible consists of 24 Books divided in three sections:

Torah = Pentateuch	Genesis (Bereshit) Exodus (Shemot) Leviticus (Vayikra) Numbers (Bamidbar) Deuteronomy (Devarim)	
Neviim = Prophets	Joshua Judges Samuel I and II Kings I and II Isaiah Jeremiah Ezekial	
	Latter Prophets	Hosea, Joel, Amos, Obadiah, Jonah, Micah, Nahum, Habakkuk, Zephaniah, Haggai, Zechariah, Malachi
CHetuvim = Writings	Psalms Proverbs Job Song of Songs Ruth Lamentations Ecclesiastes Esther Daniel	

Ezra-Nehemiah
Chronicles I and II

The three sections of the Bible are known by the acronym **T**a**N**a**Ch**, or in Hebrew תנך from their Hebrew names: **T**orah **N**eviim **Ch**etuvim. The Tanach is the Written Law given to Moses at Mount Sinai.

The Oral Law

Mishnah, Gemara and Talmud

The Written Law (Tanach) is analogous to the laws enacted by a government. For these laws to be implemented on a practical level, regulations and procedures are established by government agencies. Further detail is given by the courts who interpreted the laws. Such detail is analogous to the Oral Law.

The Oral Law was given to Moses on Mount Sinai. As its name suggests it was transmitted orally from generation to generation. Due to the dispersion of the Jews after the destruction of the Temple by the Romans, the Oral Law was codified by Judah the Prince around 180 CE as the Mishnah, in Roman Palestine. The Mishnah comprises six sections (or "orders"):

Zeraim	Seeds	Agricultural Laws
Moed	Festivals	Laws of the Sabbath and Festivals
Nashim	Women	Laws regarding women, marriage and divorce
Nezikin	Damages	Civil and Criminal Law
Kodoshim	Holy things	Laws of Sacrifices
Taharat	Purity	Laws of Cleanliness and Purification

The Mishnah is further divided into 63 Tractates. Extensive discussions of the Oral Law are contained in the Gemara. Although books of Mishnayot (plural of Mishnah) are printed separately, the Gemara is always printed with the Mishnah, each Mishnah being followed by its Gemara. Together this is known as the Talmud.

The Babylonian Talmud, compiled in 450CE includes the elucidation (Gemara) of the Jewish sages of Babylon. The Jerusalem Talmud, is less complete and authoritative, and was finished in about 340CE.

Many commentaries and derivative works on the Talmud exist. The most important of these are:

Mishneh Torah — This is a codification of Jewish Law compiled by the great scholar, Maimonides, 1135-1204, known by the acronym: Rambam (Rabbi Moshe ben Maimon -

RAMBAM). Maimonides lived in Spain and Egypt, and was physician to the Sultan. Although the Talmud is organized by subject matter, details of laws can be found in disparate sections. Maimonides took this material and organized it giving a clear definition of each law, organized by subject matter.

Shulchan Aruch — This is a further organization and codification of Jewish law compiled by the Sephardi[235] Rabbi Joseph Caro (1488-1575). This work contains the notes of the Ashkenazi Rabbi Moses Isserles (1520-1572). Thus, in one work it contains the entire corpus of Jewish law and shows, where the customs and practices of Sephardi and Ashkenazi Jews differ. This work is regarded as the authoritative source of Jewish law for all Jews, whether Ashkenazi or Sephardi.

Midrash and Zohar

The Midrash and Zohar are also part of the Oral Law. The Midrash contains collections of homiletics, parables and moral legends based on the Bible. The Zohar contains the mystical writings that are the basis for Kabbalah, the Jewish mystical tradition.

---

[235] Sephardi Jews are those of (recent) North African, Middle Eastern, Spanish and Portuguese descent. Ashkenazi Jews are those of Central and Eastern European descent. The differences between Sephardi and Ashkenazi Jewish practice do not reflect any doctrinal or theological differences. The practices of one group is viewed as equally valid by the other. Any differences should not be viewed in the same sense as the difference between Roman Catholic and Protestant theology.

APPENDIX 3: BIBLICAL DEPICTION OF THE MESSIANIC AGE

I have summarized here the main places which describe the identity of the Messiah and what will accompany his coming. The reader is invited to explore the many other Biblical references to the Messianic Era, such as the books of Isaiah, Ezekial, Daniel, Hosea and Zechariah, among others.

The perpetual sovereignty of Judah and the coming of the Messiah "Shiloh" is first mentioned in Genesis 48:10. In Numbers 24:17 Balaam foresees the coming of the Messiah at the end of days: *"a star has issued from Jacob and a scepter-bearer has risen from Israel."* The promise of repentance and eventual redemption is made by God to the Jewish people in Deuteronomy:

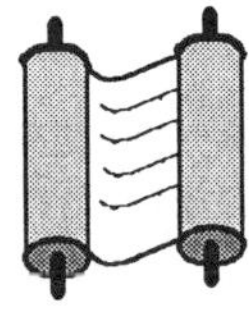

"And you will return to Hashem....Then Hashem your God will bring back your captivity and have mercy upon you and He will gather you in from all the peoples to which Hashem your God has scattered you. If your dispersed will be at the ends of heaven, from there Hashem your God will gather you in.... God will bring you to the land...." (Deuteronomy 30:2-6)

Perhaps the most famous chapter in the Books of the Prophets is Isaiah 11 which describes the coming of the Messiah from the *"stump of Jesse,"* his righteous judgment of the people and the ushering of the age of peace when the *"wolf will live with the sheep"* and a *"suckling child will play by a viper's hole."* On that day the *"earth will be filled with knowledge of Hashem."* The Messiah will *"assemble the castaways of Israel"* and *"gather the dispersed of Judah from the four corners of the earth."* The Jewish people will be reunited in peace and *"nations will seek"* the Messiah who stands as a *"banner for the peoples"* and who *"will bring justice to the nations."* (42:1)

Jeremiah 23:5-6 is more specific, describing the Messiah from the house of David, who, as king, *"will reign and prosper and he will administer justice and righteousness in the land. In his days Judah will be saved, and Israel will dwell securely."* In chapters 30-31 and 33, Jeremiah prophesies further about the reestablishment of David's throne, the ingathering of the exiles, the judgment of the people, the annihilation of the enemies of Israel, and the rebuilding of Jerusalem: *"For behold the days are coming - the word of Hashem - when I will return the captivity of My people Israel and Judah, said Hashem, and I will return them to the land that I gave their forefathers, and they will possess it."*(30:2) *"They will serve Hashem their God and David their king whom I will establish over them."* (30:9)

The lineage of the Messiah from David, through Solomon, is described in Samuel II 7:12-16,[236] with patrilinear descent established in Numbers 1:18, and the exclusion of Jeconiah and his descendants, giving rise to the Messiah being stated in Jeremiah 22:30.

---

[236] See also Chronicles I 17:11-14; 22:9-10; 28:6-7 and Psalms 89:29-38

APPENDIX 4: A SUCCAH FOR THE KLUTZ[237]: AN EASY-TO-MAKE (AND STORE) SUCCAH

Basic Principles

The Torah commands us to build a succah and to dwell in it for seven days. There are many practical Halachic[238] considerations to building a succah. It must be sited at a place where there is a clear view of the sky, not under a tree or the overhang of a house, or in a place where there is a foul odor. The walls of the succah can be made from any material, so long as they do not move in the wind. Like the shapes of the letters of the word succah -- סכה -- there should be two and a half, three or four walls. The main frame of the succah can remain standing the whole year.

The most important part of the succah is the covering, or s'chach (סכך) which must be placed each year with the intent of making a succah. The s'chach must be made of materials which grow naturally from the ground such as branches of pine trees, corn stalks, wooden beams or bamboo poles. It must have been removed from the ground. Metal wires or nails should not be used at all, neither must anything that is made from a vessel, since these can acquire spiritual impurity. The s'chach must be placed on the roof and must not be tied down, but can we weighted down with a wooden beam that itself forms part of the s'chach. Rain must be capable of dripping into the succah through the s'chach which casts a shadow over more area than the sunlight than is let through. Since the s'chach will have some openings, it is assumed that the stars will be visible.

---

[237] Yiddish for one who is not dexterous

[238] Jewish law. The outline here is for descriptive purposes only. There are many excellent sources which describe the construction of a succah and the Halachic requirements. For example: See also Torah Anthology, Me'am Lo'ez. 12:211. Moznaim Publishing, Brooklyn. 1990. Also Succos, Mesorah Publications, and the ArtScroll Machzor for Succos, (p1288).

Building a Succah

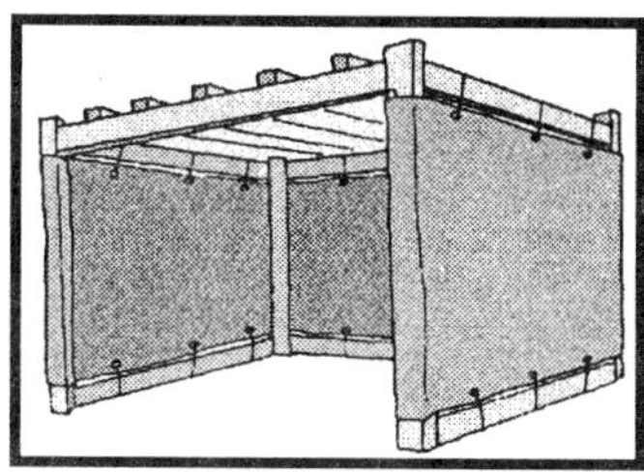

For the adventurous, your local hardware store will have all the supplies you will need to build a succah (except the s'chach - covering) like this one. You can also purchase succah kits which require various levels of construction ability. I have written down the plans for the succah my family has used since 1990. You will see how easy it is to modify this according to your own needs. The other nice thing about this design is that it can be stored easily.

You will need to gather the following:

Tools:	Hacksaw Hammer Scissors or craft knife PVC glue Plain string
Frame:	PVC Pipe (1.25" diameter - 1.5" can be also be used) 4 Uprights 2 lower lengths 2 upper lengths 2 lower widths 2 upper widths

The height should be about 6' 6"
Length and width can be up to the length of the pipe (10').

	8 L joints 8 T joints
	Up to four additional upright supports - 7'
Walls	Tarpaulin, cane mats, lattice panels (with gaps less than 3" wide), solid plyboard panels (depending on climate).
Roof support	1 x 2" pine cut to appropriate length. You will need about one every one foot of succah length.
S'chach	1 x2"s can be used as s'chach, but you will need more of them. Fresh corn stalks, pine boughs, or other suitable vegetation can be used. Alternatively, custom made

S'chach mats, made specifically for the construction of succot can be purchased and reused every year.

INSTRUCTIONS

1. Make Corner joints

Cut 8 4" lengths of pipe from offcuts. Using 1 per joint, join a T and L together so that when pipes are inserted into the joint they are mutually at right angles on X, Y and Z axes.

Joints can be made as "mirror images" of each other so that they face either rightwards or leftwards. Be sure to make four right hand and four left hand joints. Glue together.

2. Cut pipes for frame

The height should be about 6' 6"
Length and width can be up to the length of the pipe (10').

3. Additional Supports

Additional supports may be required for midway between corners (e.g. 1 per side). Length and width pieces can be cut in half and connected with a T joint. Upright supports can be connected to strengthen the structure.

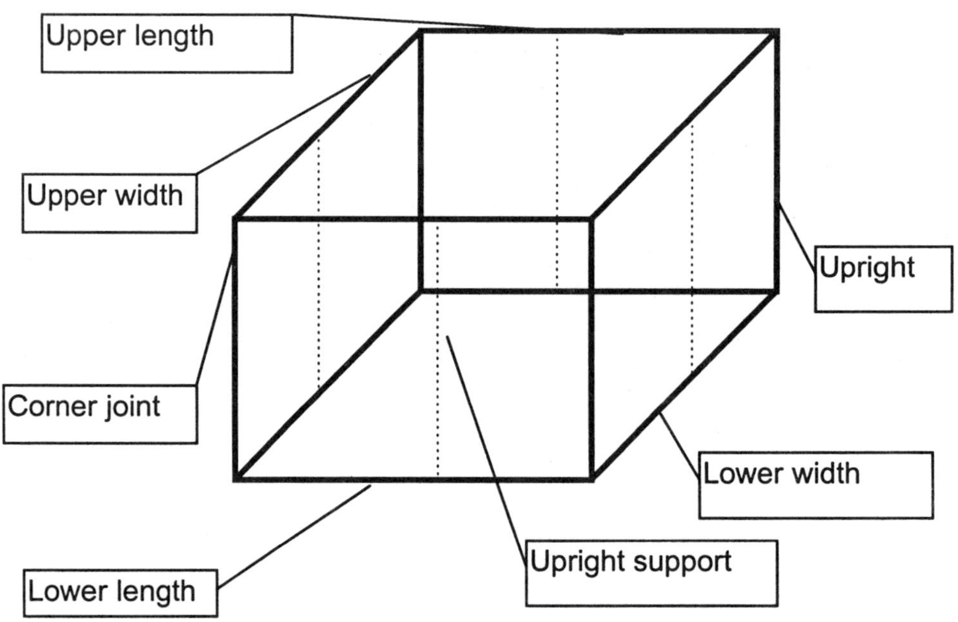

4. Assemble
Insert poles into the right angle joints you just made. Hammer gently, but do not glue. Tie to a fence for more support. Alternatively stakes can be driven in the ground at each corner to protrude 4-5'. The succah can be tied to these stakes.

5. Wall
Tarp or cane matting may be used. Tie to uprights.

6. Roof Support
Place 1 x 2's across and tie down.

7. S'chach
Place s'chach on top of roof support (do not tie down). Have in mind that you are completing the commandment of building a succah.

8. Decorate and Furnish
Decorate the inside of the succah. Pictures depicting the harvest, plastic fruit, **Zaide Reuven's Esrog Trees**, pictures of famous sages, posters explaining the laws of Succot are all appropriate. Posters of the Four Species are very popular, as are the special recitations made each day for the Ushpizin. Any part of the succah, including its decorations cannot be used for any other purpose until after Succot. Since a mitzvah - commandment must be fulfilled for its own sake (namely to do God's will), no benefit can be gained from them.

9. After Succot
The Succah is dismantled and stored for next year. Most of the parts can be used again, including the s'chach if it is made of bamboo matting or wooden beams.

APPENDIX 5: CIVIL DATES FOR SUCCOT UNTIL 2025

Year CE	Year AM	Succot 1	Succot 2	Hoshana Rabbah	Shemini Atzeret	Simchat Torah
1999	5760	25-Sep	26-Sep	1-Oct	2-Oct	3-Oct
2000	5761	14-Oct	15-Oct	20-Oct	21-Oct	22-Oct
2001	5762	2-Oct	3-Oct	8-Oct	9-Oct	10-Oct
2002	5763	21-Sep	22-Sep	27-Sep	28-Sep	29-Sep
2003	5764	11-Oct	12-Oct	17-Oct	18-Oct	19-Oct
2004	5765	30-Sep	1-Oct	6-Oct	7-Oct	8-Oct
2005	5766	18-Oct	19-Oct	24-Oct	25-Oct	26-Oct
2006	5767	7-Oct	8-Oct	13-Oct	14-Oct	15-Oct
2007	5768	27-Sep	28-Sep	3-Oct	4-Oct	5-Oct
2008	5769	14-Oct	15-Oct	20-Oct	21-Oct	22-Oct
2009	5770	3-Oct	4-Oct	9-Oct	10-Oct	11-Oct
2010	5771	23-Sep	24-Sep	29-Sep	30-Sep	1-Oct
2011	5772	13-Oct	14-Oct	19-Oct	20-Oct	21-Oct
2012	5773	1-Oct	2-Oct	7-Oct	8-Oct	9-Oct
2013	5774	19-Sep	20-Sep	25-Sep	26-Sep	27-Sep
2014	5775	9-Oct	10-Oct	15-Oct	16-Oct	17-Oct
2015	5776	28-Sep	29-Sep	4-Oct	5-Oct	6-Oct
2016	5777	17-Oct	18-Oct	23-Oct	24-Oct	25-Oct
2017	5778	5-Oct	6-Oct	11-Oct	12-Oct	13-Oct
2018	5779	24-Sep	25-Sep	30-Sep	1-Oct	2-Oct
2019	5780	14-Oct	15-Oct	20-Oct	21-Oct	22-Oct
2020	5781	3-Oct	4-Oct	9-Oct	10-Oct	11-Oct
2021	5782	21-Sep	22-Sep	27-Sep	28-Sep	29-Sep
2022	5783	10-Oct	11-Oct	16-Oct	17-Oct	18-Oct
2023	5784	30-Sep	1-Oct	6-Oct	7-Oct	8-Oct
2024	5785	17-Oct	18-Oct	23-Oct	24-Oct	25-Oct
2025	5786	7-Oct	8-Oct	13-Oct	14-Oct	15-Oct

The festivals all begin on the preceding day at sundown. Only one day of Succot is celebrated in Israel. Also Shemini Atzeret and Simchat Torah are celebrated as one day in Israel.

CE Common Era

AM Anno Mundi - year since creation, the dating system used in the Jewish Calendar

APPENDIX 6: CHRISTIAN CALCULATION OF JESUS' BIRTH AT SUCCOT

This calculation is based on the following:[239] The father of John the Baptist was Zechariah, who belonged to the priestly division of Abijah (Luke 1:5). The priests were divided into 24 groups who served in turn. The division of Abijah was the 8th course (1 Chron 24:10) who would have served at some time approximately in the middle of Sivan (May/June). Mary conceived six months after Elizabeth (Luke 1:25-31), which turns out to be 25 Kislev (November/December: Chanukah) and nine months later is 15 Tishri -- Succot.

Note that this calculation is based on the assumption that Elizabeth's pregnancy occurred after one of the five possible occasions on which her husband could have been in the Temple. An alternative calculation based on the pregnancy occurring after the second period of service (sometime in Cheshvan - October/November), brings the date of Jesus' birth to about 15 Nissan, the first day of Pesach (Passover)!

To eliminate this possibility, additional calculations have been made, based on a lunar eclipse (described in Josephus, Antiquities, XVII, 6:4, the only one described by Josephus) calculated to have been on March 13 of the fourth year BCE. According to Josephus, Herod's illness intensified and he died some time later. Only after the death of Herod could his decree to kill all males below two years old (Matthew 2:7-8:16) be invalidated, and thus only then would it have been safe for Mary to come to the Temple (Luke 2:22-38) to bring sacrifices 40 days after childbirth (as required by Leviticus 27:4). How long Herod's terminal illness lingered after the lunar eclipse is not clear. Joseph Good assumes that it was a number of months, putting the time of Herod's death in the autumn. Since Herod's death must have taken place between the time of Jesus' birth and 40 days later, Joseph Good concludes that Jesus' birth must have taken place in the autumn, at Succot, which is the only possible date calculated from the information regarding John the Baptist's birth.

---

[239] See Joseph Good (Rosh Hashanah and the Messianic Kingdom to Come, Hatikva Ministries, Nederland, TX, 1989, p161 - also at http://24.130.12.78/greg/succoth.html)

APPENDIX 7: SOURCES

Jewish Sources

ArtScroll Machzor for Succos, The Complete ArtScroll Machzor, Mesorah Publications, Brooklyn, New York

Blech B. Understanding Judaism, Jason Aronson, Northvale, NJ. 1991 Ch. 38

Bloch, AP. Biblical and Historical Background of Jewish Customs and Ceremonies. Ktav Publishing, New York, 1980.

The Messianic Era, Resurrection and the World to Come. Appendix to ArtScroll Talmud, Sanhedrin Vol 3.

Chabad in Cyberspace: www.chabad.org

Jews for Judaism: www.jewsforjudaism.org

Kaplan A. The Real Messiah. National Conference of Synagogue Youth, New York, 1985

Outreach Judaism: www.outreachjudaism.org/

Project Truth: www.utexas.edu/students/cjso/untitled_folder/Truth_page.html

Rambam - Maimonides: Hilchos Melachim (Laws of Kings) from the Mishneh Torah, Chapter 11 and 12.

Succos, ArtScroll Mesorah, (also see Simchas Torah, in the same series), Mesorah Publications, Brooklyn, New York

Weissman M. The Midrash Says: Vayikra, Benai Yakov, New York, 1982

Zaide Reuven: The Esrog, Zaide Reuven's Esrog Farm, Dallas, TX, 2nd ed. 1998

Christian Sources

Chumney E. Seven Festivals of the Messiah. Treasure House, Shippensburg, PA. 1004

Glaser M and Glaser Z. The Fall Feasts of Israel. Moody Press, Chicago, 1987

Good, Joseph. Rosh Hashanah and the Messianic Kingdom. Hatikva Ministries, Nederland Texas. 1989

John Hagee, Final Dawn over Jerusalem, Thomas Nelson Publishers, 1998

Hebraic Roots of Christianity: www.hebroots.org/

Killian G. The Watchman (contains a number of articles written from the perspective of a believer in Jesus) http://members.aol.com/gkilli/home/

Treybig et al. Holidays or Holy Days. Does it matter which days we keep? United Church of God, an International Association. Cincinnati, OH. 1999. www.ucg.org/

Other Sources

Sarachek, J. The Doctrine of the Messiah I Medieval Jewish Literature. Hermon Press, 1968, 2nd ed.

Tolkowsky, S. Hesperides. A History of the Culture and Use of Citrus Fruit. Staples and Staples, Westminster, 1937

From the same author........

The Esrog האתרוג

(The Fruit of the Goodly Tree: Leviticus 23:40)

Now in its second edition, **The Esrog האתרוג by Zaide Reuven זיידע ראובן**, believed to be the first work of its kind to focus entirely on the ....**The Esrog**...., the prized centerpiece of the *Arba Minim* ארבעה מינים (Four Species of Leviticus 23:40).

The Esrog האתרוג by Zaide Reuven זיידע ראובן is a perfect way to enhance the joy (simcha) of Succot and is packed with the history and Halacha, science and symbolism, and medicine and mysticism, of **The Esrog**. **The Esrog האתרוג by Zaide Reuven זיידע ראובן** has stories, facts and activities for the young and not-so-young, for Yom Tov (Festival) and Chol Hamoed (intervening days) of Succot.

ולקחתם לכם ביום הראשון פרי עץ הדר ויקרא כג"מ

"And you shall take for yourselves on the first day the fruit of goodly trees" (Lev 23:40)

Why **The Esrog האתרוג** ? Believed by some to be the "apple" of the Garden of Eden, **The Esrog** is the "heart" of the ארבעה מינים *Arba Minim* - "Four Species" from which, according to Jewish tradition, incredible spiritual blessings will flow if taken in the appropriate fashion.

The Esrog האתרוג must be understood within the context of the Four Species and the festival of Succot itself. The observance of the commandment to take the Four Species, radiating with the beauty of **The Esrog האתרוג**, commemorates and celebrates at once God's greatness, His forgiveness, His life-giving power, the Torah, the greatness of our forefathers and Sages, the unity of Israel and our atonement, punishment of the wicked and the restoration of the Temple. Every aspect of Jewish life and aspir--ation is reflected in the Four Species and with its observance is the promise of messianic redemption. **The Esrog האתרוג** epitomizes these aspirations and *"symbolizes the continuity of Jewish history and its common aspiration, binding together the disparate geographic units of the Diaspora over the centuries"*(Isaac & Isaac).

I looked at the etrog the golden, And dreamt of the orchards of gold,
I dreamt of the ages the olden, That never in hearts will grow old. (Raskin)

Enlarged Second Edition

As an accompaniment to many **Zaide Reuven's Esrog Trees**, this book has found its way into homes and offices throughout the world. New material in this edition adds depth to an already encyclopedic work on **The Esrog** האתרוג:

- Medical uses of **The Esrog**.
- Recipes for **Esrog** Schnapps and Candied **Esrog**.
- Recipes for **Esrog** perfume.
- **Esrog** genetics (how much of an **Esrog** is an **Esrog**?)
- Tu B'Av - 15th Av- ט"ו באב, a lesser known festival on the Jewish calendar.
- Bircat Ilanot ברכת אילנות, the blessing on seeing fruit trees bloom every spring.
- Pollinating your **Esrog Tree** and making cuttings.
- **The Esrog** and the establishment of the State of Israel.
- **The Esrog** in Christian Theology.
- A detailed map illustrating **The Esrog** trade in the 14th - 20th Centuries will escort the reader from **The Esrog** orchards of the Mediterranean to the shtetls of Eastern Europe.
- **The Esrog** האתרוג **by Zaide Reuven** has 56 pages and 298 footnotes covering Talmud, Midrash, Gematria, Halacha, Kabbalah, Anatomy, Recipes, Quizes, Stories, Internet and Botany, on.....**The Esrog** האתרוג.

PLUS: A true story of how a Russian doctor discovered **Zaide Reuven's Esrog Farm** after his assistant received messages from "voices".

The Esrog האתרוג by Zaide Reuven is written by David Wiseman, the grandson of the real Zaide Reuven.

ISBN 0-9666222-0-0

COUPONS

This coupon entitles the bearer to $5 (Five dollars) off any purchase of $30 or more from:

Lulav and Esrog Sets, Esrog Trees, Books, T shirts, Besamim Boxes, Succot (items subject to availability)

Zaide Reuven's Esrog Farm, LLC

פרדס האתרוגים של סבא ראובן

זיידע ראובן'ס אתרוג-סעדל

PMB 238, 6757 ARAPAHO, #711, DALLAS, TX 75248
PHONE: 972 931 5596
INTERNET: HTTP://MEMBERS.AOL.COM/ZRSESROG

Goods must be purchased directly from **Zaide Reuven's Esrog Farm.**
Coupon expires 12/31/2002

This coupon entitles the bearer to $18 (Eighteen dollars) off any purchase of $100 or more from:

Lulav and Esrog Sets, Esrog Trees, Books, T shirts, Besamim Boxes, Succot (items subject to availability)

Zaide Reuven's Esrog Farm, LLC

פרדס האתרוגים של סבא ראובן

זיידע ראובן'ס אתרוג-סעדל

PMB 238, 6757 ARAPAHO, #711, DALLAS, TX 75248
PHONE: 972 931 5596
INTERNET: HTTP://MEMBERS.AOL.COM/ZRSESROG

Goods must be purchased directly from **Zaide Reuven's Esrog Farm.**
Coupon expires 12/31/2002